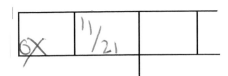

Belonging

Fate and Changing Realities

Herman Ouseley

First published in Great Britain by Hansib Publications in 2021

Hansib Publications Limited
76 High Street, Hertford, SG14 3WY

info@hansibpublications.com
www.hansibpublications.com

ISBN 978-1-912662-40-1
ISBN 978-1-912662-41-8 (Kindle)
ISBN 978-1-912662-42-5 (ePub)

A CIP catalogue record for this book
is available from the British Library

Design & Production by Hansib Publications Ltd

Printed in Great Britain

DEDICATION

This book is dedicated to all those who have experienced discrimination, harassment and exclusion and have challenged their perpetrators in order to receive justice. It is also dedicated to the people and organisations that provide support to those experiencing discrimination and for challenging all forms of prejudice, bias and institutional racism.

APPRECIATION

My thanks go out to the many people who have helped me along the way, and supported me in my efforts in pursuit of equality and inclusion. Some are mentioned in this book but there are too many to mention here. You do, however, know who you are and how much I value your assistance.

My close family members and friends have been alongside throughout my 56 years of public service. They have tolerated my challenging work ethic through all the ups and downs, which meant, more than anything, that I was 'missing' more times than I can remember. I give special thanks to all of them.

Contents

Author's Introduction 7

1. Nobody to somebody 19

2. Beyond adolescence 30

3. Work, rest and play 34

4. Stand up; speak out 43

5. Conflict, confrontation and consequences 53

6. London embraces diversity 66

7. Back to the future 79

8. A new focus; a new challenge 85

9. Unfinished business 92

10. Defying the odds and doing more with less 100

11. Promises, promises, promises 115

12. Race off the agenda 133

13. Football, bloody hell! 148

14. Hostile environment 168

15. Responsible leadership 178

16. A just society for all 186

17. Back to oblivion 198

Index of Names 203

Author's Introduction

When I began writing this memoir, it was intended only to be a revealing account of the trials and tribulations of my working life. The aim was to describe my journey through life since my arrival in Britain in 1957, and to show how I managed to navigate from poverty and insecurity to public prominence and now, back into obscurity again. However, as I began to write it became obvious to me that this volume had to evolve into something else – a more substantive account of how I was able to get into a position of some influence, despite coming from an impoverished Caribbean background. It had to tell the story of just how I got there and what difference that background may have made in contributing to my many goals.

One of the main aims of this book was to highlight some of the many obstacles I faced whilst working in public services during the post-war decades. This was a time of endemic institutional discrimination which impacted most negatively on deprived communities and vulnerable individuals. As a public servant I always tried to ensure that my efforts were targeted at identified needs and priorities. That included efforts to improve the quality, access and reach of the public services provision for the benefit of all, but especially the most-needy in society.

The central theme, therefore, concentrates on my numerous conflicts and confrontations with organisations that were extremely resistant to change. It shows some of the ways in which I tried to challenge the status quo, and attempted to overcome the subtle and deliberate obstacles which were then deeply entrenched in management cultures and processes. Above all, I intended to highlight the stark paucity of responsible leadership among cohorts of senior managers and administrators who clearly favoured personal and vested interests above a pursuance of fairness and equality for others.

Although these recollections are mine alone, they are not only about one person's experience. This memoir also reflects the experiences of many others confronted with inadequate and ineffective public services provision, and illustrates their feelings of impotency to influence change for the benefit of the neediest groups in their own communities. Over the past half-century many people of all backgrounds have gone through similar experiences to mine as they struggled to promote programmes designed to eliminate all forms of unlawful and unfair discrimination. Within this memoir, I reveal just some of those challenges and missed opportunities to tackle the causes and effects of institutional discrimination in British society.

When I left British Guiana (now Guyana), I was just twelve years old and on my way to England to join my mother. She had left her children behind in 1955 and settled in Peckham, south London, but always intended to re-unite her family as early as possible. As it turned out, I was to be the first of three to join her. Yet apart from the obvious excitement of seeing my mother again, I had few, if any, meaningful ideas about what to expect in London.

My preparation for life in the UK was minimal. At school in Georgetown, we all knew how to sing the first verse of the British national anthem, were aware of the nursery rhyme, 'London Bridge is falling down' and learned of some of Britain's kings and queens. I also knew about the Black Watch soldiers from Scotland, as they were prevalent on the streets of Guyana, assigned there by the British government to keep the peace. I spoke English, or thought

I did, until I arrived in London and soon realised that I was not easily understood by the locals.

Thereafter, south London was to be my home. Peckham, initially, was mysterious, new to me and fascinating. I became curious to understand its distinct history and more about its local working class population. Surrounded by the neighbourhoods of Nunhead, Camberwell, Dulwich, New Cross and Bermondsey, there were many places of interest to visit, with a few iconic sites. Beautiful historic buildings stood alongside many slum properties. There were visibly neglected bombed-sites and some prefabricated housing, but clearly the area was awaiting future redevelopment with the provision of permanent family dwellings.

My real fascination, however, was with the people I mixed with. They included school friends, local families and street traders. I tried hard to take in the culture of the working population, in addition to just hanging about, playing or entertaining. Urban spaces, such as those I saw in Peckham, were just at the beginning of demographic transformation with the influx of settlers from the British Empire. Although they had been invited by the British government to come to the 'mother country', these new arrivals were left on their own to negotiate and compete with the locals for housing and employment.

I struggled to make sense of it all. Resentment against newcomers was to an extent, understandable, especially as locals would frequently express their feelings loudly that the new migrants were clearly here to take their jobs and homes. Racial abuse was rife and there were many instances of violence and blatant discrimination. For many new arrivals, it was a case of 'smile, take in on the chin and move on'. Ignorance and prejudice were endemic traits of a culture fed on misinformation. Integration was talked about in negative terms. Survival meant navigating your own way through the haze of newness to find accommodation and employment, against a background with a visible colour bar. In effect, newcomers had to rely on others like themselves for help and advice. This clearly set the tone for the inevitability of segregation.

Yet, during that period in the late 1950s and the 1960s, I was always very conscious that many of the people I lived alongside and shared my schooling with were friendly, supportive and more inclined than not, to treat others with respect, decency and fairness. They were as curious of us as we were of them. There was clearly a substantial element of tolerance and putting up with each other during that period. But I clung on to them enthusiastically as they represented the best hopes for me to feel that I was a part of a local community, and among people who would contribute towards the building of a fairer society for everyone in the future.

Living and subsequently working in central London provided me with the opportunity to marvel at the history, culture and status of this great capital city. In 1963, my first job was as a junior clerk at the administrative offices of Middlesex County Council, located in Parliament Square. This was the beginning of a life dedicated to public service that would eventually span 56 years. I regarded it as a privilege to work there, and it remains a defining moment in my life. By way of historical coincidence, on that same day in August 1963, another young Black male started as a junior with the council. We never met while in employment there but we got to know each other decades later and worked on projects together in his Focus Consultancy business. Professor Chris Mullard, as he is now, was that young guy who went on to do great things in the world of education and equalities.

As I embarked on my working life, I quickly realised that to be accepted meant that you did as you were told, had to know your position as an underling, appreciate that there was a 'them and us' culture and be aware that certain parts of the organisation were out of bounds to someone like me. The class system was alive and well and there was a status-quo to be respected. Not surprisingly, I became increasingly frustrated in trying to understand how to be accepted, to gain confidence and to feel that I belonged. I observed that different treatment was dispensed on the basis of 'face-fitting' or 'liked' or 'not liked'. I continued to observe the principle that I adopted on arrival in England: Never to go where you are likely not to be welcomed, or even safe. Nevertheless, I was determined to broaden my horizons by trying to understand the different people I came into contact with and to learn from them. As a result, my personality became somewhat schizophrenic as I transformed my persona to suit the different situations I found myself confronted with on a daily basis. Essentially, it was about survival, being accepted and having perceived feelings of belonging.

Racial prejudice, discrimination, harassment and abuse were evident in almost every scenario. My whole approach from those early days was to 'swerve it', and almost pretend that the perpetrators were ignorant and not worthy of my occasional anger and rage. People would delight in reminding you that this was "their country", never the more inclusive "our country". How could you really feel that you belonged in such circumstances?

My life in public service inevitably led to confrontations with the system and its processes of power and decision-making. The system operates in a way that ensures that the powerful decision-makers dominate other people within the 'them and us' culture at work. The challenge for me was to take on that system. I could no longer be silent and ambivalent in my responses to such inequalities and discrimination. I now had to join others in being part of the solution. There would be no hiding place.

It was never going to be easy trying to challenge and eliminate institutional discrimination. From the mid-1970s, it became the central core of my entire working life, alongside my many different duties. It remains a huge challenge, even today, notwithstanding the slow steps of progress made during recent decades. My main frustration was almost always with the decision-makers themselves who thrived on the notion that change would come in due course. For me, their promises of meaningful actions were always for tomorrow, never today. That has always been the prevailing culture.

Phrases such as, "We acknowledge mistakes may have been made ... an inquiry will investigate the incidents and allegations of wrong-doing and discrimination ... take the necessary remedial actions ... lessons will be learnt," were common. They are the answers from public bodies, decision-makers and leaders when responding to actions which have had a detrimental impact on the lives of already disadvantaged and vulnerable people in society. Such promises often sound sincere and offer hope to the victims. Ultimately, however, most perpetrators of individual and corporate wrong-doing, incompetence and discriminatory conduct are able to walk away without appropriate punishment or redress for those adversely affected.

The recurrent pattern of lamentable official responses to calamitous and tragic incidents has certainly heightened awareness about the existence of institutional racism in Britain. But, for others, it still arouses indignation. The deniers reject all notions of its existence. Consistently, at such times, some commentators would question whether the consequences of on-going racial discrimination, abuse and harassment are rooted in the powerful policies and culture of organisations, or due merely to unconscious bias.

Yet, there exists substantial evidence about the extent of racial bias and discrimination. Most recently it is evidenced in the UK government's own research of ethnic disparities. Government action has always been inadequate in redressing the detrimental experiences of those who are the long-suffering recipients of unequal treatment. For example, substantial evidence of racial discrimination in policing emerged during the Covid-19 pandemic lockdown in the spring of 2020. What was the government's response? It set up yet another new 'independent' commission to inquire into the facts about racial discrimination and disadvantage. That has been the recurrent pattern of formal government responses to the continuing problems caused by discrimination for the past three decades.

The Macpherson Report into the murder of Stephen Lawrence was published in 1999, following a thorough independent public inquiry. In the light of the findings and recommendations, there seemed to be a momentum of enthusiasm to suggest that change may be on the way. Macpherson highlighted the existence of institutional racism and the inquiry findings pointed to the collective failure of the police to be racially unbiased. That was then. But, today is not much different than then. Daily reports of racial profiling by the police services continue across the country. The only real difference is that more people are increasingly prepared to use social media to expose their personal experiences of wrong-doings or observing the unfair treatment of others.

It is incredible to believe that, in this day and age, the country's leaders and decision-makers still continue to operate on the basis that you push every controversy into future inquiries, hoping that it would dampen down the clamouring for immediate action and justice for the aggrieved. And, when the reports with findings and recommendations eventually appear, they would be put into eternal further consideration without any genuine attempts to introduce change. Irresponsible leadership is attributable to individuals as well as organisations. It is the collective failure which was highlighted in the Macpherson Report. It creates, in most cases, a lack of trust and confidence in the state and its authoritative public bodies. They fail to dispense fair and equal outcomes far too often for deprived and vulnerable communities, including, and especially, Black, Asian and minority ethnic communities.

At the beginning of the 21st century, strengthened race equality legislation was promptly introduced by the government following publication of the Macpherson Report.

There appeared to be a genuine political commitment to the implementation of the report's recommendations by the Tony Blair-led Labour government, which set up the Macpherson inquiry. However, that enthusiasm was short lived. By 2005, the equality change programmes were no longer of high priority status for the government and its public bodies. The prescribed radical action needed to achieve meaningful and sustainable equality outcomes lost impetus as the government focused on other priorities, such as light-touch regulation and the war against terror.

The inner city riots in Tottenham, north London, and other urban environments across the country in 2011, provided powerful evidence of the frustration of impoverished communities. Soon to be revealed was the hostile environment of the David Cameron and Theresa May Conservative governments. The Windrush scandal, in particular, exposed the deliberately inhuman treatment dispensed to many of the families who came to Britain from Commonwealth Caribbean countries after the Second World War. They had been invited here to address the desperate labour shortages in the aftermath of the war. They had settled here and raised their families. They paid their taxes. And yet they still faced blatant state approved discrimination by often being denied access to housing and employment and from other opportunities and entitlements available to others. These 'hostile environment' policies suddenly classified many of them as 'non-British citizens' and denied them work or benefits. Some were deported; some made homeless; some detained in custody; some were made destitute; and some died. At the beginning of 2021, in spite of apologies by the state and repeated commitments to resolve all outstanding claims for compensation, there were still grievances occurring.

The past fifteen years have been frustrating for most people involved in the struggle to see genuine equality, non-discriminatory and inclusive policies in everyday activities. But, unaccountable and shameless leadership without

personal and corporate responsibility for collective failure
has remained a dominant feature in institutional culture.
It was, therefore, a welcome surprise during 2020 when
there was an apparent upsurge in acknowledging the
existence of widespread institutional, organisational and
individual racial discrimination. This all emerged as a result
of substantial media coverage of the many acts of police
brutality and killings of Black people in the United States.
Yet again, it signalled the possibility of a new dawn for
equality, inclusion and justice. The emergent optimism was
largely due to the fact that people from all backgrounds
were clearly expressing their support for actions to end all
forms of discrimination and unfair treatment. People were
taking to the streets to protest about the lack of action and
demanding justice, and there were expressions of support
for movements such as Black Lives Matter.

This memoir is being published at a time when Britain
and the rest of the world continue to grapple with the
challenges of the global pandemic. Many people from all
backgrounds, but especially from the Black, Asian and
minority ethnic communities, have been on the frontline,
particularly in working tirelessly for the NHS. This public
health emergency triggered the optimistic political refrain
of, "We are all in this together." This provided a timely
opportunity for the country to embrace the collective virtues
of people from all backgrounds, in pursuance of solutions to
this crisis as well as for equality and social cohesion.
However, the Covid-19 pandemic also created new urgent
priorities for government to deal with. Inevitably, the virus
was not going to discriminate in its attacks on people but,
equally inevitably, disparities emerged in how it impacted
on the lives of people from different backgrounds, the aged
and those with underlying health problems. Not
surprisingly, the emerging new enthusiasm promised for
action to change society for the benefit of everyone, had to
fade into the background. But, even in such unique
circumstances, it was the same familiar pattern of

unfulfilled hopes and promises being repeated. The opportunity for sustainable change did not appear as a priority for action by those with the power to do so. Instead, the promises and hopes for the emergence of sustainable race equality and justice for all would become an even lower priority. The most recent promises to provide levelling-up for disadvantaged communities had to go by the wayside, at least until the health emergency had ended. The post-pandemic priorities would, rightly, have to address the crises in the economy, health and social care services, unemployment and the national debt, all of which have an equality dimension to be considered.

There is clearly a well-rehearsed and established pattern in place to deal with race and equality crises. Whenever issues of racial discrimination, hatred and violence hit the headlines, investigations follow, action is promised, some useful projects receive support and then it is back to square one. It is reminiscent of the characteristics featured in the 1980s television political sitcom, 'Yes Minister'. Top civil servants, providing advice to ministers making decisions in crisis situations, had a formula for giving such advice. It worked along the following lines: At the beginning, they agree to say nothing is going to happen. A little further on, they agree to say something may be about to happen but should do nothing about it. At the next stage, they say that maybe they should do something about it but there is nothing really they can do. And eventually, the world has moved on, and it is too late to do anything about it. Although this satirical programme provided much entertainment and humour, it was never far from reality. It certainly continues to resonate with the 'always tomorrow' casual attitudes held by powerful decision-makers as they stifle dynamic action for desired outcomes.

Despite all of this, many Black, Asian and minority ethnic citizens have been in the forefront of campaigning for better race and community relations and for the essential action to tackle racial inequality and injustice. Many of the campaigners who came from the Caribbean, Asia and Africa are no longer with us and their enormous contributions are largely unrecorded. Historical records may not cover adequately such valuable involvement with the struggle for racial equality and justice and how they challenged individual and corporate racial discrimination during the past seven decades. But nowadays, there is at least some improved understanding and realisation of the positive contributions that such citizens have made to Britain and, in particular, their particular experiences in tackling inequalities and working for social inclusion for all. I am one of those from among the many who emerged from being a 'nobody' to become a 'somebody' in those continuing challenges to tackle all forms of institutional racism and discrimination.

ONE

Nobody to somebody

L ike so many Caribbean people in the British Colonies after the Second World War, my mother, Daphne, entrusted the care of her children with relatives and left the land of her birth in search of a better life. It was 1955 and her destination was London, capital of the 'Mother Country'.

For months I longed for her return. I would often gaze out across the Atlantic Ocean from the shores of what was then British Guiana hoping that one of the passing ships or overflying planes would be bringing her home. But she didn't return. .

I was eleven years old and had led a relatively sheltered life. My father, who I had hardly known, was dead. My mother had left me and my two sisters and moved to England, so I was living with my Aunts Birdie and Josephine.

My days were a mixture of running errands for a few cents a time or regular instances of school truancy, much to the dismay of my aunts. . I was always either fetching or carrying something! I did anything from gathering coconut shells to assist neighbours with the construction of pathways to their flood-affected homes, to collecting discarded empty drinks bottles and returning them to Jonnie, the friendly Portuguese bartender at the rum shop. The financial rewards provided the entry fees into the cinemas that showed the latest John Wayne westerns, among others.

One year after my mother's departure, my world would change forever. My aunts, apparently so fed up with my waywardness, announced that I, alone, would be leaving British Guiana to be re-united with my mother in London. My head was in a spin of both bewilderment and excitement. I was about to take a monumental step into the unknown, and a new life thousands of miles from home. I left British Guiana on the 14th July 1957 on a short flight from Georgetown to Port of Spain in Trinidad. This first stop was for two nights, after which I embarked on the cargo and passenger liner, *SS Italia*.

I was now just twelve years old, travelling alone and excited by everything I saw. I was enthralled by the magnificent expanse of the Caribbean Sea and the Atlantic Ocean; experiencing new insights into life among my fellow passengers day after day. I carefully observed the other travellers and learnt how to get by without being shown. It was this self-sufficient trait that helped to shape my life; how to learn from others and understand their needs.

The long and arduous journey also played tricks on my mind. On a number of occasions, while staring in wonder at the seemingly endless ocean, the devil in me teased and invited me to jump overboard! My obsession with the sea was perhaps drawn from my life back home where I was surrounded by water; whether it was the rivers, the canals, the ocean, or the regular floods that occurred in Georgetown.

After brief stops in Madeira and Santa Cruz in Tenerife, I arrived in Genoa, northern Italy on 30th July. Then it was onwards by train and ferry across the English Channel, and finally another train journey to London. It had been an epic solo journey for someone so young, but the end was in sight and I was going to be reunited with my mother. She was a devout Anglican and I knew that she would have prayed every day for my safe journey. I finally arrived at Waterloo Station where she was waiting for me.

Mum was a woman of resolute and unshakeable faith, despite the problems in her early life. Most significantly, the fathers of her three children were absent long before any hopes of developing meaningful relationships.

Nevertheless, she had trained as a nurse in Guyana, but on arrival in London had to settle for a variety of low-paid jobs such as cleaner or carer just to make ends meet. She also had to raise the necessary funds to pay for my passage to England, since my aunts had told her that I was getting out of control and becoming too much for them to handle. Her original plans were to eventually move from London to New York, but my challenging behaviour and my impending arrival meant that these plans were dashed.

Just seventeen days after leaving British Guiana, I had arrived in London. The culture shock was immediate and I was totally bewildered by it all. I was really excited to see my mother but, never a demonstrably affectionate woman in public, there was no warm embrace. I assumed that she was still angry with me for my misbehaviour back in BG and, therefore, spoiling all her future plans. However, she didn't hold this against me until later in life when, on many occasions, she would express regret about missing the opportunity of moving to the United States, where other family members had settled. Now there was also a new man in my life to relate with, something that was novel. Her soon-to-be husband, my new step-father to-be, Egbert, extended his welcome.

Within a few weeks of my arrival I was being kitted out in uniform to attend the William Penn Secondary School. This school was located in nearby affluent Dulwich but its pupils came predominantly from the working class areas of Peckham, East Dulwich and Nunhead in south London.

A year later, my two younger sisters, Doris and Desiree, followed to join the family. They had a much more straightforward journey by air plane from British Guiana to London. By the time they had joined up with the family, I had already gone through a whole set of new experiences in order to adjust and fit in with my new life in south London.

Being called a 'wog', 'choc-ice', 'sambo' and 'coon' by other children with smirks on their faces may have seemed like fun, but I was naively unaware that I was being racially abused. They smiled mockingly and I responded in similar fashion. However, it really hit me hard when, not long after, some local adults confronted me in the streets to tell me, "We didn't win the war for people like you to come here and take our jobs and homes." Little did I know that they were as ignorant as I was about the facts of our mutual history. That included facts about the African, Asian and Caribbean contribution to Allied forces during the two world wars, as well as their status as British subjects, citizens and residents of the UK. I also quickly learnt that the 'KBW' graffiti on the railway bridges meant 'Keep Britain White' and was the slogan of the British Fascist Movement.

Having developed survival instincts on my solo journey to the UK, it was now necessary for me to learn how to cope with and overcome the hurt of racist abuse. When you are out-numbered you don't pick a fight. That was the easy and safe option, but, I still had a lot to learn. What was racial prejudice, why was it so rampant and how did it contribute to discrimination and hatred? Why was the UK government complicit in permitting overt racial discrimination, and why did it fail to utilise all aspects of education to reduce the levels of ignorance on such matters?

My new domestic arrangements in Peckham were less than basic, but I did not know that other neighbours were much better accommodated. I was sharing a bed with my mum and new step-father in a multi-tenancy end of terrace house, where we were renting one bedroom and another multi-purpose room. Everything else was shared – the tin bath in a utility room, external toilet, sinks and stoves on each landing and paraffin heaters to provide heating when needed.

I was lucky to find a very friendly Scottish family living opposite us in Choumert Road, Peckham. They seemed fascinated by my arrival in the neighbourhood and, unlike some others, were genuinely welcoming. Within days they arranged to take me to a military tattoo in Woolwich, which was a new and exciting attraction for me. It was a real treat to be feted with such warmth and friendliness. The event itself was, no doubt, executed with precise military efficiency, but I was more interested in getting to know the family as they struggled to understand my accent and me theirs. Disappointingly, some six months later, they moved to another part of south London, and I never really got to know them as much as I had hoped.

A key priority for my mother was for me to link up with the local parish church, St Saviours. This church was in Copleston Road, only about 100 yards from our home. I duly joined the choir and later became a server but, after six years, I found a new pre-occupation when Sunday morning football became my new focus for 'worship'. My mother was, not surprisingly, displeased. However, when I shattered my knee on Clapham Common fourteen years later I started to show an interest again in St Saviours and later would help raise funds for its conversion to a centre for multi-faith worship, a day centre and nursery school.

Although I was clearly an outgoing and friendly youngster with my school friends I had a secret that I did not share with any of them, and that was my home life. The only school friend I was not ashamed to invite to my home was Robin Barnfield, known affectionately as 'Barney'. I often went to his home in Camberwell for a cup of tea and snacks, and we played football in the streets and local parks. We also rode our bicycles all over London, discovering the locations of the London football clubs. To hide my embarrassment about my impoverished living conditions, two other good school friends, Alan Watkins and Bob Insley, were never invited to my home. Nevertheless, Alan and I have stayed in touch with each other since we first met in 1957, and he and another friend from William Penn School, Terry Peters, were my security when I started to venture into the so-called 'Den' – the stadium of the legendary Millwall Football Club. Back then it was located at the appropriately named Cold Blow Lane.

The perceived shame and embarrassment I held about my home life proved hard for me to reconcile and influenced how I saw myself in this new life, how I saw other people and how I imagined what they were thinking of me and my lifestyle. My own bias and ignorance about other people, despite knowing little about them, would have been the dominant factor in determining how far I would allow people into my life. My sheltered life moulded me into being very private and reserved, and it was difficult for others, however friendly, to be able to understand who I was. In truth, I struggled to have any coherence then about who I was and what my life was all about, other than doing what I was told and deciding how to survive the challenges of each day.

Everything in my life was now new and exciting, and adapting to situations was always challenging. Coping with things necessitated the acquisition of different personas so that I could feel comfortable with the demands of the contrasting cultures and environments. At home my persona was what it needed to be for the folks originating from Guyana, speaking in a dialect that was strange to the locals. In south London I had a face and style for school, another for the street and others, as required, depending who I was meeting and how I felt I wanted to be perceived. Nowadays, racial and ethnic identities and issues of Englishness and Britishness still pose challenges for Britain's multi-ethnic and multicultural communities. Back in the late 1950s, it was about adapting my personality to suit every eventuality. I wanted to be liked, to be loved, to belong, to be accepted and respected. But, even then, those were all fanciful feelings and emotions. Prejudice and racism were factors all the time, even though I had no deep or significant awareness of what it all meant in reality, other than having to bob and weave around difficult issues as they arose. I was responding instinctively to new situations, struggling to grapple with anything that was not straightforward and making things up as I went along. I felt that, as an outsider, you might be acceptable on the surface but I could not truly belong because "you are not one of us". This was a recurrent theme of life through the decades to date.

It was essential that I learned to understand the environment in which I found myself – where to go, who to speak to and who to avoid eye contact with, as well as how to be comfortable with strangers and befriend or avoid them. Fortunately, avoiding eye contact was easy for me, as it was a family trait from the earliest recollection of my childhood. My school life was dominated by trying hard to be accepted, and doing stupid things to attract attention and gain popularity among the other boys who enjoyed 'mucking about'. Kicking a football around the playground was also new to me, as there was no football in my life as a child in Guyana. The dominant sports, from colonial times, were rugby and cricket. These led me to an understanding of apartheid, because virtually all the serious participants were white Brits and, until the late 1950s, the West Indies Test cricket team was largely made up of British expats residing in the Caribbean islands.

At first, when football teams were being assembled in the school playgrounds, I knew that I would always be the last to be selected, not because I was not liked, but because I was useless and of little value. I had speed, agility and athleticism, but no technique or co-ordination between my brain and my feet to help me connect with the ball. However, by the time I left school in 1963, my enthusiasm for playing could not be denied and I was usually among the first to be chosen for matches. It took me quite some time to reach the required standard but I enjoyed the sport so much that I made it my priority to become better each week, month and year.

I also fully appreciated the importance of education, as my mother had drummed this into my head from when I was a small child; she always encouraged me to be enthusiastic about and understand the value of reading, writing and arithmetic. But, inevitably for someone wanting to be liked, I was more interested in the joys of mucking about and often joined others in being disruptive, thus deflecting from serious academic studies.

This misconduct often got me into trouble. At school being caned by a teacher was regarded as a badge of honour. I can remember our geography teacher, 'Kipper' Kirby, always entered a chaotic classroom, greeting us with a loud "Quiet!" When things calmed only a little, he then indulged in mild sadism by shouting, "Who wants the slipper?" This was an invitation for him to slap your backside with the soles of rubber plimsolls, and he was always rewarded when several hands would be raised, including mine; he would then become even more enraged, temporarily losing self-control and self-respect.

More serious were the few occasions when my mother received a letter from the headmaster, George Dennis, asking her to attend the school to discuss my behaviour. My dear mother was working day and night for a pittance to help sustain the family and, as a generous, family-loving person, she was also supporting needy family members in Guyana with regular remittances. I remember affectionately how pleased I was to receive my five shillings postal orders from my mum during the year we spent apart. So she would be very angry to be summoned to the school, as she would have to take time off work and lose pay. That was bad news for me as she would give me several slaps for my alleged misconduct, then a few more for receiving the letter. There would be more admonishments on the way to school, and then she would administer a few more whacks across the head in front of Mr Dennis to prove that she regarded my misconduct seriously. This was in addition to the punishment already administered by the headmaster, usually several strokes of the cane against the backside. Nowadays, that would amount to a form of brutality, but in those days even I regarded it as deserved! And, just when you thought that was enough, she then gave me another few slaps when she received her pay slip, and found it to be less than usual because of the time she had taken off work because of my misdemeanours.

A defining moment in my school life at William Penn was when my housemaster, Mr Holman, took action which resulted in me getting one of the biggest hidings of my life. One day the school tannoy system announced, to my astonishment, "Would Ouseley please go to see the housemaster, Mr Holman." Off I trotted, full of anxiety but unaware of what was awaiting me. Holman was a giant of a man, perhaps 6ft 5in tall, with a deep, bellowing voice. He wasted no time. "Come in, boy." "Thank you, sir," was my response. He then went for it. "You were seen smoking on the platform of North Dulwich station last night." I wanted to say that many other boys were doing the same but, when asked for an explanation, I said nothing. "Well, if that is your answer, drop your trousers." He grabbed the cane and gave me six lashes on my backside. It did hurt, but my pride was even more wounded. I went home that evening, did not even consider the desirability of a cigarette (proof to me that smoking was only to be flashy and to be one of the boys, rather than necessity) and I never mentioned any of it to my mum to avoid double punishment.

The next day, at almost precisely the same time, the same announcement came across the tannoy system. "Would Ouseley please come to the housemaster's office, now." Oh my God! I was trembling with fear. My backside was still a bit raw from the previous day's lashes. My brain was in overdrive as I tried to recall any misconduct that I would now have to account for. "Hello sir, you want to see me," I whispered. A broad smile appeared on his face. I thought for a moment that this guy must like indulging in caning rituals. Then his appearance changed as he spoke. "Ouseley, you are wasting your time at this school. I have been thinking that you need to take more personal responsibility for meaningful involvement in school activities and I am now making you a prefect."

What the hell had I done to deserve this? The feelings of pride and apprehension came in equal measure over the prospects of my new role. With badge on blazer and emboldened with responsibilities, I would be the one barking out instructions to get the boys to line up for lunch and for classes. So far, so good. But when the school day was over, and unknown to me, my initiation ceremony awaited at North Dulwich station. A group of boys armed with sticks gave me a right going over for joining the other side, wearing the prefect badge and pushing them around. Some of the beating was accompanied by racist taunts and insults which were more painful than the cuts, bruises and swollen arms and legs. There were too many attackers to fight back and, eventually, they ran off. At home, I explained my disfigurement by attributing it to a violent rugby match and my mother offered no sympathy. I thought of trying to get my revenge against each of the boys because I believed they deserved it, although I had no enthusiasm to do this myself. I imagined that I would have been physically capable of taking them on individually but abandoned the idea. This change of heart was dictated by my absolute belief that all forms of violence against the person should be opposed. So, thank you Mr Holman for encouraging me to take on responsibility. I got a severe beating for my efforts to meet the challenge you set me, but it was a pivotal moment for me in accepting that there was a right way, a wrong way and another way of living your life, rather than satisfying the need to feel one of the boys.

Having acquired a more serious focus on school life and its purpose, I realised how much catching up I had to do in order to leave with a modicum of success and achievement. Suddenly, I found myself awake in the early hours – 3 or 4 am – swotting and preparing for exams. It was now down to me. Only I could make the difference between success and failure, and taking personal responsibility for this was my driving force. It was around this time of my school life that I began truly to understand the meaning of 'perseverance' and the importance of never giving up, no matter how hard, or easy, this might be.

The power of perseverance was most meaningfully demonstrated when, eventually, I was selected to play football for the school team in a competitive game against another local school. Our opponents were more skilful and stronger, and I said to our sports teacher at half time that I felt that my performance had been abysmal. He was not playing me in my best position and I hoped he would change it, but he simply told me to persevere. I did; he was right and my second half performance was better. We still lost but I had improved through perseverance, and his belief in me also helped. Another lesson had been learnt!

TWO

Beyond adolescence

As school life came to an end, my thoughts turned to work, ongoing studies and the next phase in my life. My main desires were to be independent, make my own decisions, earn some money and do my own thing, though I was still unclear what that was to be. But all of this was merely an aspiration and, perhaps, even more so an illusion and fantasy. The key elements of my life were work, study, play football, cultivate friendships and partying. Music and football were my main passions then and remained so to this day, along with family and friends. But over the years, tackling inequalities and taking on voluntary and charitable activities have over-ridden most of my time.

My mum influenced my early musical tastes, but she was deeply upset that I put to one side my duties at St Saviour's Church in preference for the local playing fields and kicking a ball around endlessly. Giving up the church and not pursuing my piano playing were unforgivable in my mother's eyes, as she nursed secret ambitions for me to join the clergy or, at least, be the church's resident organist.

She was, however, reassured that I was sound in my choice of friends. All my close friends were either former school mates or known local boys and, later on, work colleagues who were happy and comfortable with me in their presence and spaces. My concern about personal safety and security meant that there were many self-imposed no-go areas in south London and elsewhere, where I knew or suspected that I would not be welcome, even when invited or accompanied by friends. Still to this day I remain cautious about the places where I am prepared to go because of perceived or real concerns about personal safety.

I always exercised suspicion and cautiousness and seemed somehow to possess a natural instinct for survival. I enjoyed my own sense for perceived comfort, and stuck steadfastly to the principle of never going anywhere I thought that I would not be wanted or welcomed. There were several pubs, clubs and local places that some of my friends frequented and enjoyed, but I never felt a sense of loss or resentment when choosing not to join them. I was always conscious of who I was and how, rightly or wrongly, people saw and judged me. Although I was conscious that racism was a factor, I did not have a full grasp of what fed racism, such as historic slavery, oppression, power and racial prejudice. I was fully aware that I was scrupulous when determining in my own mind how I perceived myself, how I thought others saw me, how I saw others and how this affected my interaction with other people in any given situation. There were choices always to be made, decisions taken and the consequences to address, but self-preservation was a strong motivator.

My two best neighbourhood friends at this time were Clive Simister and Carl Douglas, both of Jamaican heritage. Clive was very handsome, dressed stylishly, and was a fabulous footballer whom I admired as much for his skill and good looks as well as his charisma. He was always full of joy and fun to be with. We played football together and Clive, who was as strong as he appeared, was always polite and endearing in his manner although he could also be either brutal or gentle in competitive sport. He loved his blue beat, ska and reggae tunes, which I did too, but I was overwhelmingly partial to my mum's own taste in music: blues, gospel, calypso and classical tunes. These all became my main musical preferences.

Carl lived with his mum, Ruby, in the street next to mine in Peckham, and was even more musical than me and Clive. Some two and a half decades later, he had a number one hit with the popular, self-penned 'Kung Fu Fighting' making him an overnight pop sensation. In our day-to-day friendships back in the 1960s, Carl performed at a couple of the iconic, late night Soho venues in London's West End and occasionally, I would tag along. My problem was getting into those clubs as they had exclusive memberships, which were beyond my 'status' and affordability. However, we found a way to get me into one of my favourite venues, The Bag O'Nails in Kingley Street. Carl and I both drove Austin Minis, and would travel separately to Soho to arrive at about 11 pm – my usual bedtime! When we parked up I would carry his bags, having been designated as his 'clothes manager' for the night. The artists' dressing room was always in a 'fog'. I had given up smoking cigarettes some years before while still at school, but this was a whole new experience. Everyone knew that I was 'clean' so the joints being passed around were never offered to me. I did, however, puff on the odd cigar every once in a while, posing in my dark glasses as though I was a 'somebody', rather than just a mere observer. It was an exhilarating time, spotting the stars I had previously only ever seen on television.

One night in 1970, I encountered one of my idols at The Bag O' Nails – the legend that was (and still is) Jimi Hendrix! He was dressed in his now iconic style: the hat; the leather jacket; the guitar in its case and slung across his body. He approached the table where Carl and I sat and said, "Let's go and split a joint, Carl." They both headed off to the back rooms, leaving me behind. I felt abandoned but, at the same time, in awe at having been in the presence of the great Jimi Hendrix. I sat there for what seemed like ages, dumb-struck. Shortly afterwards, they both emerged, no doubt feeling somewhat chilled.

Hendrix then joined Carl up on stage for a brief appearance before making his exit. A few weeks later, the music world was rocked by the announcement of his death on 18 September 1970. A bit of magic went out of my life, as it did for so many others across the globe. I never went back to The Bag O' Nails, and saw Carl rarely thereafter. He moved on with his musical career, performing on the international stage and continually on tour.

My life was also moving in a different direction. One light might have dimmed a little as Jimi departed from the live music scene, but the ongoing reality and vibrancy generated from the music and the football worlds still flowed joyously. This was 1960s London and it was not called the swinging sixties for nothing. Rapid changes in culture, fashion, food, music and outlook were taking place. For those of us growing up then, irrespective of your race, sex, class, neighbourhood or personal circumstances, it was a time to go with the flow. Excitement was there in abundance if you wanted it or to make it to suit yourself, family and friends.

For a period of around 18 months in the mid-1960s, I regularly frequented the Black Prince pub in Bexley, Kent, on Sunday nights with my school friends, Terry Peters and Alan Watkins, from our local football team Conlon United. It was here that we saw stars such as Rod Stewart, Spencer Davis, Zoot Money, John Baldrey, Chris Farlow and other up and coming musical artists of that generation. Their music was aligned to my taste with its roots in the Black music from the USA and very much based on vintage blues, soul and gospel. Seeing Georgie Fame live at the Flamingo Club in Soho whetted my appetite for what was to follow – Otis Redding, Aretha Franklin, Eddie Floyd, Wilson Pickett, Isaac Hayes, Sam and Dave, Atlantic, Stax and the whole Tamla Motown extravaganza. I was absorbed in all forms of music but I was a 'soul man' at heart. I created a small self-styled mobile disco, and played at a few small clubs and other gigs. I also occasionally involved myself in a few jam sessions, singing, but with no particular ambitions other than growing up, enjoying life and searching for whatever niche might take my fancy.

THREE

Work, rest and play

L eaving school in 1963 meant abandoning adolescence, making a choice about a career and starting to think seriously about adulthood. I wanted to go into personal care services but my first application for a job did not even yield a response. Luckily, soon after this, I found another opening and, after interview, was offered a junior clerk position with Middlesex County Council in Town and Country Planning administration – a whole new world for me. I was based at the council's administrative headquarters, the Guildhall in Parliament Square, a building which today is the home of the Supreme Court. I worked in a team led by two incredibly talented women, who commanded the respect of the chief officers and their subordinates. I reported directly to a solicitor, John Smith, and the other junior clerk in the office, Stuart, reported directly to Vic Bailey. Vic was a keen smoker and Stuart, even as a junior, smoked a pipe. The cramped office of four was often smoke-filled in those days. Stuart and I made tea and coffee, washed up, undertook errands and deliveries and did filing, Gestetner printing, copying, collating and dispatching. We were the juniors and we knew it; but we were grateful to be there learning and earning, both money and respect.

I threw myself into it with enthusiasm, full of delight to be in work, desperate to do well and hungry to learn more about the policies and processes of local government. The more I did the more I was given to do, until there appeared to be an unfair division of the workload between Stuart and myself. Over time, it became clear that John and Vic were happy to delegate more to me because I had demonstrated, through my care, attention to detail, willingness to learn and the extent of my output, that they could trust me more than my counterpart. Stuart, on the other hand, was very laid back and regarded by the bosses with diminished enthusiasm. Their apparent trust and confidence enabled me to develop a desire to undertake further studies in local government, and I enthusiastically embarked on a correspondence course.

At that time, in 1963, a thirty-year roller-coaster career in local government was not something I envisaged. I was more interested in find out how I could get off the bottom grade to the next level. But before I could get moving onward and upward, the government of the day, as often happened during my local government career, decided to re-organise London local government. Middlesex County Council and the London County Council would be abolished and their responsibilities merged as part of the creation of the Greater London Council (GLC). In April 1965 I was absorbed into the GLC's workforce and assigned to land charges duties. Somehow, through dedicated work, I would finish my daily tasks by lunchtime and then was bored for the rest of the day. After a few weeks of this I decided it was not for me as there was no challenge, no learning, no development and no future.

My colleague there, Peter Edis, who became a good friend, was even more laid back than my previous colleague Stuart and took everything in his stride. But, he was great fun and a lovable colleague. Some days he and I would wander off for a lunch break in the local pub and a visit to the bookies to take a punt on the horses. He was a Chelsea supporter and a good footballer himself. A few years later we both played for my local team, Conlon United, and we travelled together to Old Trafford to watch Manchester United play mid-week European Cup night matches. Peter was tremendously shy, reserved, lacked some confidence and was the most easy-going guy I knew; so laid back that he often forgot to come to work! On one occasion, when he did not show for work, I phoned his home to see how he was. His mum said that he was at work but, in fact, he had spent the day at the local library!

Within weeks of deciding that my GLC position had no future, I made a successful application to join the Development Control team in the Department of Architecture and Planning of the London Borough of Hackney. Here I continued to learn and amass more experience in planning administration. Working in and around Old Street, the Angel and Dalston took me closer to the realities of street life and the stressful situations so many people were facing. Understanding discrimination, poverty, deprivation and social needs, and how these were, or were not, being met became priorities for me. Nine months later, this understanding provided me with a platform from which to apply, successfully, for an administrative officer's job with Lambeth Council. This was closer to home, so there would be less travel and there was also the prospect of more learning, personal development and, hopefully, good times.

Although I was delighted to get the post at Lambeth, I was surprised to have succeeded when I later realised there was a 'sitting tenant' already in the office with the expectation of being anointed into that vacant post. Fortunately, my boss to be, John Bland, took a shine to me and fought a good fight to get me appointed. He genuinely believed in, and fought for, equality and fair treatment in recruitment processes and practices. However, three years later, we would be finding ourselves on opposite sides when selecting a candidate to head an old people's home.

I started the new assignment at Lambeth in June 1966, and the challenge I immediately faced was to win the confidence of my new colleagues in my ability to do the job and also to prove that John Bland's decision to champion my appointment ahead of the intended incumbent was the correct one. I knew the only way I could do so was to get my head down, concentrate on getting the job done and blend into the culture of the office environment. I was now much more adept at being a Black face in a white working environment and culture, and I could move in and out of that culture without feeling too uncomfortable. There would always be times when things were being said that I would turn a blind eye to, however much I found it to be distasteful or embarrassing. I did not possess the confidence or courage to challenge such outbursts or to engage in arguments or discussions. That was then, and I was not yet sufficiently prepared or educated to fight and win those battles. There were other more immediate priorities for me to address.

Winning over Jim, the unsuccessful combatant for the post, presented me with an even tougher challenge. He appeared resentful at first and did as little as possible to be helpful, but I was grateful that he eventually came round and I felt there was a grudging, if unexpressed, respect for my work ethic and forbearance. I do not think that my race, colour or youthfulness were the primary reasons for his resentment; rather, there was an expectation in Lambeth's office culture that an insider was entitled to be appointed to the vacant post. As doubters were won over my position was enhanced, and my boss, John, who had given me the opportunity to thrive, felt vindicated in having stood up to his boss who clearly did not want me there. The job itself was not too demanding and I enrolled in a day-release course to pursue the Local Government Management Diploma at Catford College in south London.

In the planning teams Jack Peters, Alan Turner and John Trotter, among others, became my buddies. We all played football and this was the glue that bonded us, although bar billiards and the local Tosca for a lunchtime fry-up were also activities that brought me into the fold. John Trotter stood out among them all and we have remained the best of friends ever since. He and I played and watched football and travelled to different parts of the world, and I became part of his cabal of friends who supported Chelsea, including, notably, Jimmy Hare, Alan Knights and Micky Leech. There were also Ray, 'Spud', Woody and Arnie, although they gradually became detached from the group in recent years. At one stage we were self-dubbed the 'Seven Tops' but nowadays we are more like the four and occasionally three tops. Nevertheless, we are all still fantastic close friends.

Another person who had a significant and lasting impact on my life was Chris West. He joined Lambeth around 1968 as a management trainee. He was a south London boy and we often joked about our respective schooling for, while I went to the local comprehensive, he got a scholarship to go to nearby Alleyns Public School. My school was nicknamed 'Billy Biro' instead of William Penn by the boys at Alleyns. They had allowed their pupils to leave early each day to avoid our pupils confronting them on the way home. Chris introduced me to some of his close buddies, including Mark Callanan who was his best friend and became a good friend of mine. Chris was a very popular guy; he was loveable, down to earth, larger than life and a genuine person who cared about others. He had a band of followers and, nearly two decades after he passed away in 2000, we still try to meet at least twice a year to celebrate our continued existence and reminisce about the wonderful times we had with him.

After a few years working in Lambeth town planning, the development control administration had become routine. Although I had no direct contact with him whatsoever, I was disenchanted with the hierarchical supremacy of the distinguished Director of Development, Edward Hollamby. Ted, as he was warmly called, especially by those in the world of architecture, was undoubtedly a well decorated individual, who commanded respect among fellow professionals. However, it appeared to me that he, along with a few of his trusted lieutenants, appeared to have their own agenda to change the entire landscape of the borough to satisfy their own egos and achieve their profession's acclamations and architectural design awards. But, to my knowledge, they rarely ever expressed publicly any empathy and genuine concern about the deprived people of the borough. They were well paid to serve as public officials; their priorities, from my perspective and concerns, were for the aesthetics of the buildings constructed and their impact and visibility on the landscape rather than people and their needs. These chief officers were virtually unchallengeable in the 1960s; even the elected councillors had to yield to their much flaunted expertise. Their approaches to planning and development appeared to marginalise the importance of democratic decisions and local people's views. Compulsory Purchase Orders to facilitate large redevelopment projects often meant displacing families and breaking up communities and neighbourhood cohesion. Whilst some such comprehensive redevelopments were necessary to clear slum properties, there was an absence of planning for people first, rather than satisfying planning policies. The priority for the council in matters of redevelopment and housing should have been identifying what people's needs were and how they could be met. These considerations should have been taken seriously before making decisions and over-riding officers' approaches where there was the apparent dominant attitude of, "We know what is best for you".

It was not a part of my remit to challenge such decisions. There was neither requirement nor reason why I should have concerned myself with how the council at the highest level was running as an enterprise. But I could not detach myself from being more focused on people than infrastructure, land and buildings. As a result, I became frustrated and disillusioned. This began affecting my enthusiasm for the work so I took the plunge and decided I needed to learn more about the local people and their needs. I knew about the history, structure and operation of local government services from the perspective of the provider, but less about the views and requirements of the local population. I felt, as an insider, that we were driven by regulation and process. I was spending time telling people what they should do rather than helping them find solutions to problems and achieve satisfactory outcomes for them and their communities. For example, a recurring concern was the difficulty that many householders were experiencing in getting grants for bathrooms and indoor toilets. This was a real gripe of mine, seeing people so frustrated with bureaucracy and its systems of administration. Perhaps I was particularly peeved because, from my own personal experience at home in Peckham, we were desperate to have an indoor toilet!

My next move was into Lambeth social welfare services. When I joined in 1969 it was being transformed and absorbed into a new, wide-ranging social services directorate. My job was in part to look after the residential needs of elderly residents for whom we had statutory care responsibilities.

My immediate boss was a tall, sturdy guy, Vernon Shergold, who was steeped in an old fashioned local government culture. He was very straightforward, very welcoming and likeable, and was helpful in enabling me to learn the basics of the job quickly, which I was excited to do. I was also lucky to be reunited with John Bland, who helped to recruit me into Lambeth Planning back in 1966. He was now Shergold's boss as the principal adult services manager, responsible for the entire spectrum of day care and residential adult services. This was a job I instantly learned to love and, as I reflect back over my entire employment career, I know that it provided my most satisfying experiences, both personal and professional.

I worked with exceptionally dedicated staff, mainly local women of Irish and Caribbean backgrounds. They cared for the residents who were infirm and disabled, mostly aged over eighty years. Each required continuous care and attention, and they got it. In those days Lambeth Council was very progressive – moving away from large, institutional homes for the elderly and developing purpose-built homes, with both single and double rooms. These provided residents with the opportunity for personal independence, where possible, as well as privacy and dignity along with quality care and devoted attention. Residents' family members were so impressed with the standard of accommodation and high-quality care that they often asked how soon they could book themselves in, and said that this was where they would want to be when their own time came. Social care of the elderly, the disabled and the vulnerable was a high priority then, but has gone downhill since those halcyon days, with successive governments over the last fifty years continually downgrading it.

As adult homes officer my job was varied, and I gained more understanding of the local people's social needs. The job entailed employing and managing staff, planning budgets and monitoring expenditure and cash flow, preparing inventories and equipment orders and accounting for supplies and liaising with designers, decorators and furnishers. I had to do this against a background of hierarchical structures which, at times, were still rooted in a command and control type of management.

By 1972, I realised that I still had much to learn about the essential needs of families, neighbourhoods, individuals and community organisations in the borough, and was anxious to improve my knowledge and understanding. I still had a very carefree lifestyle, enjoying my band of friends, was passionate about playing and watching football, running my mobile discotheque, singing in clubs and pubs occasionally, holidaying abroad and generally enjoying life. But I was soon to be married to a very special person who was to become my best friend, and I would have to face up to the responsibilities that go with family life. There was a growing sense that a changing lifestyle lay ahead. Should I change the job that I loved and had become good at? I could do it with my eyes closed, so to speak, but I was ready to take on greater responsibilities with enhanced earnings, even if there would be less personal satisfaction and enjoyment. The moment of change was around the corner, but when it came its arrival took me totally by surprise.

FOUR

Stand up; speak out

At the beginning of 1973, the social services adult homes division was preparing to open one of its new adult homes for around fifty elderly residents and had interviewed applicants for the position of head of the home. There were two of us on the interview panel – John Bland and me. After interviewing several candidates we agreed there were two excellent individuals, who were both appropriate for appointment. Although this position was advertised openly, the two best candidates both already worked for Lambeth in different existing adult homes for the elderly. I was asked by John for my assessment of them both and my reasons for identifying the proposed one for appointment. My boss said he agreed with me but those upstairs (meaning his boss, the assistant director) had decided that the other candidate was to be selected. I was furious with him and he knew that I would be, to find myself in such an unacceptable situation. I told him that to proceed on the basis of such a discriminatory instruction would be wrong and unfair, especially to the candidate who was entitled to be appointed. I never understood exactly why the hierarchy would give an instruction to appoint their chosen person, instead of the best candidate following interview.

I concluded that the higher up you go on the ladder of seniority, the more the appointments are made based upon face-fitting considerations, rather than the best candidate for the job. Clearly, the whole processes would have been a waste of time and I wanted nothing to do with it.

A few days later I was admonished by those at the top for, "Causing trouble and questioning orders." That was it – time to move on again. It was an era where you make your point, if you feel sufficiently principled, knowing that the implications and repercussions would result in becoming branded as a trouble-maker, having your cards marked and damaging any future career prospects. Clearly it was time for me to get out! And I had an idea which I thought would suit all parties.

It was agreed that I should take up – at my request – a secondment in the sphere of community development to expand my awareness of local people's needs and learn more about how best to respond to them. This short-term opportunity was quickly converted into a permanent post as the administrative manager of Lambeth Council for community relations. This position had previously been the preserve of the former local Town Clerk, John Fishwick, who served as a part time honorary general secretary prior to my arrival. At the time the Community Relations Council had a Chief Community Relations Officer, George Greaves, who was a war veteran with service in the RAF and a member of the Windrush Generation, having come from Guyana to settle in Lambeth. Because I too originated in Guyana we were soon designated as members of the 'Guyanese Mafia'.

It was my job to carry out all the administrative responsibilities such as raising income, personnel management and providing infrastructure for developing community-based and community-led projects. Our joint task was to promote harmonious community relations by building better race relations in the borough across different racial groups. At that time, increasing clear racial tensions were emerging in inner city areas such as Lambeth and, in particular Brixton and surrounding neighbourhoods. There were settlements of residents who were born in the Caribbean and who had migrated to Britain in the post-war period at the invitation of the government, to assist with the revitalisation of the economy and to fill gaps in the labour market and key public services such as the National Health Service (NHS). These new settlers had aspirations to make better lives for themselves and their families. However, their arrival had clearly generated a background of some resentment, hostility and blatant racial discrimination.

At that time racial discrimination was not unlawful. There was British Movement graffiti with statements such as, "Stop immigration; start repatriation," racial attacks, outbreaks of neighbourhood conflict and confrontations, deteriorating police/community relations, and blatant discrimination with notices such as 'Rooms to let: No Irish, No Blacks, No Dogs' or 'Job vacancies: No Irish, No Blacks/ Coloureds'. There was also politically inspired race hatred and, in 1968, then Member of Parliament and Shadow Defence Secretary, Enoch Powell's notorious 'Rivers of Blood' speech had created fear and tensions and would have contributed to the hate. There was massive support for the views of Enoch Powell, which added to the climate of fear. My life, and that of my family and many others, was filled with anxiety as a result.

Black families and individuals in the Lambeth borough lived, initially, mainly in private rented houses in severely overcrowded conditions or, if in council owned property, accommodation that white families refused to occupy. The main areas of discontent in the locality were discrimination in housing, employment and education, and conflict between the police and sections of the Black African/Caribbean community which especially affected young people. At the Community Relations Council we had a responsibility to deal urgently with this blatant racial discrimination and disadvantage, but little or no effective powers were available to us to challenge the discriminators until the enactment of the 1976 Race Relations Act. This created the Commission for Racial Equality, and enabled our local Community Relations Council to be transformed into the Race Equality Councils, including Lambeth.

During my seven years with the Lambeth Community Relations Council, I was very fortunate to work with and learn from some formidable and talented individuals including George Greaves, Gloria Cameron, Miranda Hyslop, Judy Weleminsky, Ansel Wong, Francis Maclennan, Gerlin Bean, Olive Morris, Tony Ottey and others. I also worked with, and among, significant operators in local communities such as George Berry, Rudy Narayan, Jay Thakker, Rene Webb, Courtney Laws and Darcus Howe. Local self-help groups emerged to meet the concerns of people who had experienced discrimination, been denied access to opportunities or needed help in dealing with conflicts.

Many people were making positive contributions by challenging racial discrimination, educating the local population about Black history and culture, providing personal counselling and advice and engaging in action to achieve equal and fair treatment. Desperately needed counselling and advisory services were provided by bodies such as the Brixton Neighbourhood Community Association, led by the impressive Courtney Laws. His organisation uniquely also had a significant focus on making provision for senior citizens' care and meeting some of their needs. Courtney Laws was one of the most prominent local figures in Brixton and was undoubtedly known by most Black people in the local area. He had been active as a young man from the moment he settled in Brixton in the 1950s from Jamaica and was reportedly providing leadership for other recent arrivals seeking refuge in the Lambeth area. He was exceptional in promoting better community relations and became the voice of Black people when the authorities had to be challenged about their failings and their discriminatory treatment. He was also prominent in contributing to national initiatives to tackle racial discrimination, and promoting good race relations in other parts of the country.

Courtney walked the streets of Brixton every day and was always smartly-dressed, or 'suited and booted', as we would say. He attended every meeting in the borough that involved community and race relations, and always with something to say. However, he did attract some resentment and jealousy from others who considered their own views as more important. There was also a new emergent generation of leaders among the young people of Brixton, who were also anxious to assert their views as being more relevant in the front line of deteriorating police/community relations.

Another prominent organisation based in Brixton during the early 1970s was the Melting Pot Foundation led by Rene Webb - another war veteran from the Windrush Generation. This organisation worked to address the needs of homeless and unemployed young Black people. They were also vital alongside other local youth and community workers in liaising with, and supporting, the many disaffected Black youngsters, especially those encountering members of the local police force. The organisation operated along informal lines, often providing cash to young people for meals, bus fares and other essentials. It was a practice that ran counter to the norms of the authorities, who sought to formalise and control the operations of such grass-roots organisations. But the priorities of these groups were to be on the streets, tackling problems head-on and to engage with the young people in whatever ways were deemed most effective. The disaffected youth wanted no dealings with the authorities!

Police and community relations were fragile in Lambeth, as well in other parts of London and the major cities throughout the UK. The widespread and disproportionate use (and abuse) of the 'sus law' (a police stop and search law to target 'suspicious' persons), particularly against young Black men, created an atmosphere of anger and fear. The police wandered the streets, often in plain clothes, looking for 'suspicious' persons to apprehend.

Police practices included rounding up young Black people, detaining them with no justification and subjecting them to racial and physical abuse. Our community relations office, other community groups, advice centres and the Lambeth Law Centre received numerous complaints from people claiming that the police had framed them or had planted 'evidence' upon them. The police were also accused of brutality, corruption and possible collusion with actual criminals, and the use of tactics to provoke retaliation which would lead to arrests and charges. They were accused of taking schoolchildren off the streets of Brixton and Stockwell and detaining them at police stations in neighbouring boroughs. On many occasions, we learned of parents returning home from work only to discover that their children were 'missing'.

The fact that almost all of those apprehended were Black was apparently of no concern by the Metropolitan Police hierarchy or the Home Office. This hostile atmosphere sowed the seeds of deep mistrust, fear and hatred of the police. Local Black residents were in no doubt that the disturbances were a direct response to the aggressive and racially-motivated actions of the police.

The local policing culture in Brixton and the surrounding areas at that time had many people from the ethnic minorities feeling uneasy and fearful. Many law-abiding folk, myself included, were always extra careful when on the streets, knowing that we were all regarded as suspicious and were vulnerable to random and unwarranted arrest.

One Monday morning in February 1977, just after 8 am, two young men, aged around 30 years, came into my office at the Community Relations Council, which was on the third floor above a furniture shop in Brixton. They were dressed in jeans, trainers and bomber jackets, and I thought they were maintenance workers. They asked if I knew the man who had just walked through my office. I said, "Yes, he is a colleague of mine, Sid." They wanted to have a word with him, and I took them next door to see him. They immediately said that they were arresting him and asked him to accompany them to the police station. When I challenged them and asked why they were arresting him they showed their identity as police officers and revealed that they were looking for a Black man, wearing a sheepskin coat, in connection with a stabbing over the previous weekend at Clapham Common.

Sid was shorter than me, was darker in skin tone, very quiet, a devout Christian and harmless in my eyes. He was visibly petrified. I told him I would accompany him to the station. It was snowing lightly outside so I grabbed my coat, ran after them and, as I put it on, one of the officers remarked, "You have a sheepskin coat as well, so you better come along with us." That was my intention anyway. My duty was to protect and support Sid, as best as I could, from the sort of inappropriate treatment he might get once at the station.

When we arrived I was told that I, too, was under arrest. We were both relieved of some clothing and possessions and placed in a cell. That was a new experience for both of us, but we now had confirmation of the policing style that many others were experiencing on a daily basis. I was as sure of Sid's innocence as I was of mine but we were well aware of the many allegations of stitch-ups, corruption and abuse. Nevertheless, the police made it clear to me that they were hell bent on 'nicking' any Black person wearing a sheepskin coat, and asked me if I knew any others. Unbelievably, and perhaps stupidly, I told them that I had another colleague, Lloyd, who also wore a sheepskin coat. Guess what? They arrested him too. I don't think he was pleased with me!

Fortunately, as we were walking along Brixton Road to the police station, I had been able to get word to people on the streets about Sid's arrest and possibly mine too. It was not long before a group of local people were protesting in the snow outside the 'cop-shop' calling for our release. When the police hierarchy realised who they had arrested (i.e. me, a 'somebody'?) they quickly tried to release me, with an apology indicating that they should not have detained me; it was a mistake and I was free to leave. I refused to go without Sid as I knew he had no case to answer. They duly accepted that they had no basis to detain Sid and released him; no doubt due more to the presence of the demonstrating crowd outside the station and the individuals who had reported the matter to Scotland Yard chiefs. It was a crazy situation, and it was hard for people outside of that environment to believe that the police would arrest people without reason. Eventually, over a period of several months and through the voluntary work of local community solicitors and supporters, we sued the police and finally got our apology and a token financial settlement. We were lucky, but we knew that many others would have worse experiences than ours without any justification, an apology or compensation, and creating a legacy of hatred of the police for the indignities and injustice heaped upon individuals and communities.

During the late 1970s, street crime was rife and the police deployed the Special Patrol Group (SPG) in areas such as Brixton. Its officers seemed to operate to their own rules, picking people up randomly and detaining them unnecessarily. They were often in plain clothes and appeared happy to be dressed like street thugs so as not to be recognised as police officers. They harassed young Black people, used stop and search and 'sus' laws, often without reason, justification and most definitely without any accountability. Prior to the Brixton riots in 1981 the police introduced 'Operation Swamp' with the objective of tackling increasing criminal activity in the borough of Lambeth. Tackling street crime was necessary; but having scant or no respect for innocent people and treating all Black youth as potential criminals was a high-risk strategy likely to result in conflict and confrontation. The 'sheepskin saga', as mentioned earlier, was a relatively small but typical example of irresponsible, unaccountable, corrupt and unprofessional policing.

The day when Brixton went up in flames in April 1981 was a strange experience for me. It was a Saturday morning about 8 am and I was heading to Lambeth Town Hall to conduct some job interviews. I travelled down Railton and Atlantic Roads, which were regarded as flashpoints in terms of the clubs, the 'shebeens' or people just hanging around on street corners. I expected it to be quiet (it was); but it was exceptionally eerie, and this atmosphere haunted me all day. I still felt the strange atmosphere after the interviews had finished and as I travelled back home. I was also feeling unwell with oncoming flu symptoms. I was resting in bed at 7.30 pm that evening when I got a call from the Chair of the Lambeth Council Community Affairs Committee, Councillor Stewart Lansley, who said, "Get down here, Brixton is burning!" My immediate thought was, "No chance!" Brixton was indeed burning but I was also overheating with influenza! The rest is history. I recovered in time with the help of medication, but the Brixton community took much longer to recover and, four years later, it was again under siege, with rioting against alleged police abuse and misconduct.

The disturbances were not unexpected. The local Black community felt that the rising levels of police harassment would lead to some form of response or reaction. However, the intensity of the anger was a symptom of the many experiences of unfair and hostile policing suffered by members of the Black community. Young people, in particular, joined in as they saw this as an opportunity to let the police know that they had had enough harassment and discrimination and they were determined to fight back.

Community relations were already on a knife edge, but what could no longer be avoided was the reality that Black people were making it clear that there would be no peace without justice, fairness and equal treatment of all people.

Community relations and race equality were now high on the agenda, at least in theory, if not action. In 1979, I had left the Community Relations Council and re-joined Lambeth Council, to head up its newly formed Race Relations Unit and to be the council's principal race equality advisor. Shortly before that, the Opposition Leader, Margaret Thatcher, had raised the temperature of debate on immigration and race relations with her notorious 'swamping' speech. This was a decade after Enoch Powell's 'Rivers of Blood' speech and it undoubtedly added to the existing levels of hostility and hate. Inevitably, there was adulation for her from others who welcomed her comments. That speech set the toxic tone for the forthcoming general election which elevated her to prime minister for the next decade and more.

FIVE

Conflict, confrontation and consequences

T he local political scene in Lambeth was geared up for change. The ruling Lambeth Labour Party councillors had set out a radical agenda for redevelopment, homes, social care, jobs, community development, leisure and recreation. Significantly, they had also pledged an end to all discrimination, especially against disabled people, women, Black, Asian and other minority groups and other disadvantaged communities. This was their promise at the 1978 local council elections. A number of other local authorities across the country, but particularly in London, had similar manifestos in which they prioritised meeting local needs and providing better services and opportunities for the poorest sections of their communities with a focus on gender, race and social class.

Being on the front line of local politics, even though I was not a politician, was all new to me and, having operated at the margins for years in championing action to end inequalities, I was now being propelled into a position of relative power.

As head of the first Race Relations Unit in local government, my principal tasks were to devise, with consultees, a race equality strategy along with an operational programme to tackle disadvantage and get the council to focus more effectively on promoting good race relations across the borough. Like it or not, I was now part of the system and part of the problem. Therefore, I was tasked with the clear aim of seeking solutions and gaining the support of the community, politicians and senior officers for my proposals and recommendations. One of the first tasks was to identify allies who were empathetic, had knowledge of the system and an understanding of its discriminatory characteristics and who could connect effectively with sympathetic politicians. Without such backup and support the project was doomed to fail.

Initially, there was much scepticism. Some people regarded the initiative as simply tokenism. They argued that, compared to the relative powerlessness of being on the outside, on the inside you were marginally better off, but you still only held an advisory role which meant no-one need agree with or even listen to your proposed actions. Above all, if managers and their staff were not implementing the policies, if there was no ownership, auditing, monitoring and accountability of the implementation programmes, there would be no credibility for the work of the Race Relations Unit. Cynicism, whilst understandable, was not easy to overcome, and could only be done by building trust and confidence and earning respect by delivering change. The reality was, and always is, that effective change happens in the public sector only when there is accountable political leadership and support, coupled with committed and responsible management at all levels of the executive to own and implement the equality policies and programmes.

Whether you are in or up against 'the system' you are dealing with organisational arrangements, operational structures, processes and bureaucratic procedures underpinned by rules and regulations. These processes are controlled and applied by managers, practitioners and administrators whose attitudes, actions and priorities ultimately determine who gets what, where and when. They have real power and can use and misuse it according to how much they can get away with, in line with what they consider to be reasonable and justifiable on their own terms. This is how institutional discrimination flourishes. In

Lambeth the power was in the hands of men, with very few women in similar posts and no Black people occupying any key decision-making positions. The decision-makers had no authentic understanding of Black people's needs nor, in most cases, any interest in finding out what these were. As far as they were concerned there was no inequality or race or gender discrimination as everyone was treated the same. They had no interest in understanding that their 'colour-blind' and 'treat them all the same' approach was discriminatory in its impact and outcomes. It was such blatant racial discrimination that led the newly elected Lambeth Council to set up the Race Relations Unit to bring order and accountability to the administration. We were tasked to develop policies and practices that would achieve equality outcomes and fair treatment for all residents in the borough – in theory.

For the first time in history a local authority was moving away from ad hoc initiatives to tackle inequalities, plumping instead for comprehensive corporate policies and practices across all its activities. Everything the council did would have to be assessed for the race, gender and disability impact. Consideration, prior to decision making, would always in future be given to the race, gender and disability dimensions in order to identify and eliminate any adverse equality consequences or impact. It was also necessary to implement compensatory measures in the form of lawful positive action to overcome historic and current discrimination, and to eliminate institutional and social disadvantage. Such equality initiatives were, of course, denounced by central government and media commentators as 'positive discrimination', and ministers would regularly and publicly reject the notion of quotas for minorities when, in fact, none were ever on offer nor proposed. The fact that 'positive discrimination' was already unlawful and not being pursued seemed to go over their heads, and their rejections were aimed at explicitly discrediting the equality initiatives.

Section 71 of the 1976 Race Relations Act had placed specific duties on all local authorities to 'make appropriate arrangements' to ensure that their activities were undertaken with due regard to the elimination of racial discrimination and to promote equality and good race relations among different racial groups. However, at that time most local authorities did not take the duty seriously. Equality was not a priority requiring explicit and additional activity because of their 'colour blind' approach. When challenged about compliance with their statutory race equality duty they would respond by indicating that they had considered 'making appropriate arrangements' in accordance with the duty and decided to do nothing. It was, therefore, mere exhortation without punishment or sanction. But how could 'do nothing' be acceptable? In the early 1980s a working party set up by the central government's Department of Environment revealed the deficiencies in the implementation of Section 71, and set out improved advice to local authorities. This was more well-intentioned exhortation from another level of the civil service hierarchy, but it was merely a nudge in encouraging those who had any inclination to pursue equality policies and practices to do a bit more.

Lambeth Council's response from 1979 was to pursue comprehensive equality programmes. Initially, it gave priority consideration to race, gender and disability discrimination and disadvantage by identifying the extent of the problem and implementing action programmes and structural reforms. The emphasis was on engaging better with local communities, particularly those described as 'usually excluded', powerless and living in relative poverty. The introduction of local neighbourhood councils aimed to get services and facilities closer to the people and devolve decision-making. Shifting power away from top heavy bureaucratic structures was now a high council priority. The recently elected council comprised some very powerful members, who were determined to take control, to be directional, to lead and push decision making where they felt it would have greatest benefits for local people's needs.

In reality, however, this 'devolution of powers' was delusional. Providing small grants and allowing some provision and control of facilities was the extent of the 'power shift'. Clearly, it was a move in the right direction but, in effect, the local and neighbourhood decision-makers were well known political and social activists who had close relationships with the politicians making the decisions. For instance, handing over control of communal facilities, such as the use of tenant halls and other resources on a housing estate enabled a local tenants' association, led by a powerful trade union organiser and party member, to run the facilities in a way that maintained the status quo. This often, at its worst, excluded Black and Asian families and individuals. But the new regime would ultimately be challenging such bad practices with its equality programmes.

The council itself had no elected Black members at that point, although the electorate would, in time, change that profile. As an employer, less than six per cent of the council's workforce was Black/Asian and they were mostly found in the lowest grades or the least desirable jobs. Women were also underrepresented in senior positions and opportunities for people with disabilities were minimal.

Addressing this problem and putting arrangements in place for fair, open and accountable recruitment practices required urgent negotiations between the Race Relations Unit, management and the trade unions. This was undertaken with each service director on a one to one basis. It was often a tortuous and painstaking process, with much denial of discriminatory practices when challenged. They would ask you to produce evidence to show discrimination but would never, themselves, be able to produce any evidence to demonstrate what actual equality existed in their directorates.

One of the best illustrations of what the Race Equality Unit was up against can be gleaned from the discussions with one of the biggest employment departments at that time, Construction Services. With the exception of Shell UK and the Greater London Council at County Hall on the Southbank of the Thames, the council was the biggest employer located in the borough. It had many major redevelopment sites and an extensive house building programme intended to meet some of the acute housing needs of local families and homeless individuals. The director of construction services held a clear view that no discrimination occurred in his department when confronted by me. However, he was unable to account for the invisibility of Black and Asian staff among his office-based staff and diverted attention to 'blue collar' employees, claiming that we should look at the on-site recruitment arrangements where, it was suggested, unfairness might occur. Even though those employees were part of his directorate, he seemed to absolve himself from any responsibility for any possible discriminatory employment practices by diverting me away from himself. It demonstrated the gap and disparity between white and blue collar workers, even in such local services. Nevertheless, I agreed to pursue his helpful suggestion, as every area of opportunity to end discrimination had to be exploited.

In following this up I was asked by the convenor of the shop stewards for the construction services directorate to attend a meeting of all stewards to explain what the council had in mind with its equality policies, programmes and practices, and their implications for his department and his members. I readily agreed.

At that meeting, attended by myself and colleague Daniel Silverstone, we were greeted by around twenty-seven male stewards of whom one was Black and nicknamed 'Chalky'! The convenor opened the meeting with the following introductory comments:

"Brothers, this is Herman Ouseley. He is from the Race Relations Unit. There is no discrimination here. He can ask our brother Chalky in the front row here who could verify this. We go to all of Chalky's boxing gigs and support him. Ain't that right, Chalky?" 'Chalky' nodded obediently. "So if you think you are going to come here on Monday morning with a truck load of niggers onto our building sites and tell us we have to take them on, you have another fucking thing coming!"

He was cheered enthusiastically by the 'brothers', including 'Chalky'. We were not able to match his rhetoric but achieved an agreement to keep talking, and persevered with a charm offensive to try to sell the proposals on a win/ win basis. We argued that everyone would benefit from fair practices and the elimination of racism, sexism, nepotism, backhanded friendly favours and back door entrances for those they knew and the exclusion of those they did not like. Eventually, persuading politicians to change policies and practices with facts and evidence won the day. They could see how opening up opportunities would also be beneficial for white candidates who were being denied fair treatment because of the ingrained nepotism and closed recruitment networks. Over the ensuing two-year period, before I moved on in 1981, considerable progress was made to institute changes in policies and practices.

The Lambeth model became a template for eradicating institutional discrimination from local authority functions and activities, but could only really be effective if there was political buy-in and the will to push changes through. We were fortunate in Lambeth to have strong political leadership on these issues from recently elected councillors who made up the ruling administration. Without the responsible and committed leadership from the top by the council's leader, Ted Knight, and his committee chairpersons, progress would have been limited and would have confirmed the community scepticism which greeted the initial announcement of the setting up of the Race Relations Unit.

Some of the senior executives in the council regarded the equality initiatives as necessary and demonstrated an enthusiasm for fairness but, in the end, would always back their key staff, strategically and organisationally, in finding ways and reasons to object, reject, obfuscate and undermine proposals for change coming from the Unit. Initially, they rarely ever put forward their own proposals to help the council achieve its objectives. They would listen to and consider the advice we offered, but did not always take proposals and recommendations on board, without prevarication. Even worse, there were employees down the line with excellent ideas and initiatives who were overlooked and not allowed to contribute.

Tokenism was something that all public service bodies across the country exploited by having the visible single Black face in different departments and regarding that as evidence of equality progress. I always regarded myself as one of those 'tokens' who had to succeed for the benefit of others to follow. To fail was not an option in moving forward and the very prospect of failure was the driving force to succeed. Success required collaboration and inclusion, and no token could succeed without others joining together with commitment to the changes needed to bring about fair practices for all. But inclusion in those days was a dirty word and a non-existent concept, so there was little or no opportunity to gain formal buy-in from junior staff other than through behind the scenes and informal networking.

During the years 1979-81, the route to ultimate success in implementing equality programmes was a reporting and accountability structure in which the head of the Race Relations Unit reported concurrently to the chief executive, the leader of the council and the Community Affairs Committee, which was the lead committee for race and other equality matters. This sent out a powerful message to the organisation that support, ownership and responsibility for driving change was coming from the most powerful sources in the organisation. To facilitate a consistent approach across all of the council directorates, each chief officer was held responsible and accountable for the equality implications of all their activities and were required to incorporate in their committee reports an assessment and analysis of the likely race equality and race relations implications and expected outcomes of any proposal.

This unique model was the forerunner to what was to be introduced two decades later, following the Macpherson Report into the murder of Stephen Lawrence in 1993. Two decades after Lambeth's radical structures were in place, the Race Relations Amendment Act of 2000 set out the requirements of the Public Sector Equality Duty, including the production of equality schemes and equality impact assessments aimed at identifying and eradicating structural and indirect discriminatory systems, procedures and processes. Even then it was seen as too much red tape and regulation by some senior executives and public body leadership, yet in Lambeth the template had been introduced back in 1979.

These radical approaches to tackling inequalities in Lambeth at the end of the 1970s and the early 1980s reflected the political stance of the newly elected councillors at that time, but the council required additional resources to give effect to its expansive social programmes. As such, it soon came into conflict with central government over its defiance in relation to the rate-capping regime it wanted to enforce. This was an era of some high-spending local authorities that supported programmes to meet local acute social needs, as opposed to central government that wanted to constrain public expenditure. Councils such as Lambeth were seen as irresponsibly spendthrift, whereas others, like neighbouring, Conservative controlled Wandsworth, were viewed as paragons of economic prudence. Many argued that the government loaded the rate support grants to favour Conservative-run local authorities and, conversely, to strangle Labour-run councils through the denial of independent decision-making. Such comparisons were politically helpful for the government, but did nothing positive to highlight relative disadvantage and the needs of people living in impoverished areas.

An example of the problem faced by Lambeth Council in responding to the acute needs of its population was in the area of housing. In 1978, the council's newly elected housing chair acknowledged that there was a mismatch between housing supply and demand, to the extent that people with desperate housing needs had no choice of tenure and were part of a growing lower income group reliant on public sector housing provision. There was also racism within the housing market and the council's housing allocation policies and practices. Against this backdrop the government was pressuring the council to cut back spending on its current and capital programmes.

The Race Relations Unit, through the work of Dan Thea who was based in the Housing Department, evidenced, through research, the existence of both direct and indirect discrimination in housing policies and practices. However, highlighting race and housing problems and suggesting solutions led to the emergence of many conflicts. Local white residents were encouraged to lobby their councillors on the basis of fears that Black households and homeless families would receive preferential treatment. The reality at that time, however, was that no Black families received offers of accommodation in any modernised or newly built dwellings. Their allocations were predominantly older, often sub-standard, accommodation that had been rejected by white households. The issues were complex insofar as housing needs and housing entitlement were concerned. Inevitably, and understandably, many local white households felt that their families, their long-term residencies and their neighbourhood connections entitled them to the best accommodation, and priority over the needs of households regarded as newcomers and undeserving, irrespective of their housing needs.

Dealing with such competing demands and the associated emotional complexities required considerable negotiation skills and sensitivity. Consultation was undertaken and working groups set up with the aim of educating staff, tenants and politicians about institutional discrimination and how it could affect all sections of society, albeit in different proportions. In addition, there were neighbourhoods and housing estates that were regarded as 'undesirable' where 'hard to let' units were, inevitably, snapped up by homeless families, who had little or no alternative choice. The downside of this arrangement was to allow people to wrongly blame the concentration of homeless families in poor accommodation for creating ghettos and labelling the residents as 'undesirable'.

The challenges were enormous, and it was enlightening and uplifting to see the council's political leadership facing up to conflict and confrontation. They were up against a government that was hell-bent on controlling and reducing the level of public expenditure on essential local services, in some areas irrespective of the overwhelming deprivation and disadvantage. In seeking to eradicate discrimination and bring about more equitable access to much needed public services, some progressive local authorities were branded as 'race traitors' and 'nigger-lovers'. People like me were occasionally called 'Uncle Toms' who were serving their masters.

The process of institutional change required a number of complementary and, sometimes, conflicting approaches, however. Our emphasis was always on fairness for all and helping individuals to gain an understanding of the need for change, both personally and institutionally, and the benefits this could bring to all communities. In trying to change prejudicial attitudes, a priority had to be getting individuals to accept that they had a duty to comply with lawful equality policies and practices even if they did not agree with them; they had to treat people fairly, even if they did not like them. Over a longer period of time, as different racial groups mixed, the benefits from sustained equality policies and practices applied effectively and fairly would become more apparent and acceptable to most people.

From 1979 to 1981, it was an intensive period of activity for me, driving this programme of change and learning as we went along. I had fantastic assistance from committed colleagues in the Race Relations Unit including Dan Thea, Daniel Silverstone, Mary Wells and Valerie Amos. The work required perseverance, continuing negotiations and tactical operational skills to bring about institutional and personal changes across the directorates of town planning, administration and legal, health and consumer affairs, housing, civil engineering, economic activity, amenities, construction, finance, personnel and social services. By the time I left, in April 1981, to take up a similar assignment with the Greater London Council (GLC), much organisation and cultural change had been achieved. The Black and Asian workforce had doubled to twelve per cent, then to 24 per cent. It continued to multiply year on year after my departure, as there was a sustained momentum for change. That momentum was crucial then, as subsequent experiences over the past four decades have shown that progress made without intense sustainability can soon be reversed, thus proving the resilience of institutional discrimination if unchallenged.

The newly introduced open recruitment procedures and practices worked effectively, and one example of how this improved the organisation's performance was in the construction services department, which, initially, had been opposed to transparency and change considered to be unnecessary.

When open recruitment and positive action were first considered within the construction services directorate during 1979-80, the clearest and starkest imbalances were in apprenticeships and trainee opportunities. Only thirteen out of the 117 apprenticeships were held by Black young people. Management put forward a number of reasons for this, saying that Black youngsters did not want apprenticeships and so did not apply for them; that Black youngsters did not want to pursue a three or four year study course; and that Black youngsters who did apply failed the Construction Industry Training Board (CITB) test. Girls and young women, it was claimed, had no interest in working on building sites but in reality they were never encouraged or considered suitable as applicants.

The action programme agreed by the Construction Services Committee in February 1980 had the twin aims of maximising the number of Black applicants for the apprenticeship intake that year and ensuring that the selection procedures were absolutely fair. All existing closed and preferential entry methods were to be eliminated. At the time of this recruitment drive, the directorate was fortunate to have appointed a new Apprentice Supervisor, Reg Morrison, who was totally committed to the council's goal of equal opportunity for all, and he was a key person in the implementation of these new procedures. For the first time, a wide network of community organisations was trawled and the vacancies were advertised within local schools, in the Black and Asian press, in the careers service and among local organisations, including Black, Asian and other minority ethnic groups. The local youth responded; 306 applications were received and, after careful consideration of each, 151 applicants took the CITB test, of which fifty-one (or 33 per cent) were Black or Asian. All those who passed the test were interviewed and twenty-four applicants were offered apprenticeships, of which eight (or 33 per cent) were Black or Asian.

This clearly showed that Black and Asian young people do want jobs, do want apprenticeships and, if encouraged, will apply for these opportunities. Furthermore, the quality of apprentices in the new intake continued to improve and young men and women from all backgrounds had the opportunity to become qualified professional staff in subsequent years.

SIX

London embraces diversity

Becoming the first ever head of the Greater London Council's new Ethnic Minorities Unit was a step into a bigger terrain of activities, and fertile territory in which to bring about change. The GLC was responsible for most regional services across local borough boundaries such as transport, strategic housing provision, highways, waterways, the arts and culture, economic development and historic buildings, along with the management of a considerable property portfolio and land banks. However, the perception of many Londoners was that this massive regional authority and its public service activities was remote from the reality of the struggle on the ground to gain access to personal, social and community services for those with unmet needs. It seemed closer to central government and its civil servants than to London borough councils and their residents.

In 1980, the newly elected GLC, led by Ken Livingstone, wanted to rid itself of this remote outlook and image. It wanted to engage with London's populace, particularly around job creation, and invest in services to tackle unemployment and meet social needs, especially in the poorest parts of the capital city. This administration was seen as radical in its approach to public expenditure and the expansion of public service provision. It had been the subject of media interest and interrogation from day one, especially for the way it had ousted its previous elected leader, Andrew MacIntosh, for the new incumbent, Ken

Livingstone. It declared that it would ultimately make London a low cost public transport zone and reduced fares in 1981. However, this suffered a setback when, as a result of a legal challenge brought by south London's Bromley Council, the courts ruled that it was illegal as the GLC was acting outside its powers. The main news media was very critical of Livingstone and some of his colleagues, and daily reports aimed at discrediting the administration received disproportionate coverage, particularly in branding the council as irresponsible and extreme.

My own personal experience of a hostile media was chilling for me and my family immediately after I joined the GLC. I had received regular abuse from all sorts of people and groups while at Lambeth trying to tackle inequalities, with complaints coming from all political standpoints as well as from community interest groups. This, I realised early on, would be inevitable when you put yourself in the front line to challenge the status quo and those with power. Criticism included being regarded as unworthy of being in a position to challenge those with status and privileges by setting out programmes and projects aimed at securing a fairer society for all. In my two years as head of the Lambeth Race Relations Unit my worst experience was over a period of some weeks when I received telephone calls, usually in the middle of the night, which were either silent at the other end or threatened with the chilling statement: "We know where you work; where your wife works; where your kids go to school."

I would be subject to yet more sinister threats when I took up my post at the CRE in 1993. I received bullets in the post which provided a further reminder of the potential for violence against me but also against my family; another reason why my family's low profile was, and remains, a priority.

Should I have walked away then? I was consumed with fear but emboldened by the people who had died for civil rights and justice around the world, and I thought all the time of this conflict in my life. My overall priority was always to protect my family, and when I reported the calls to the police I was advised to change my number; this I refused to do. I agreed with my wife that she would not answer the phone. When I was at home I would answer, instantly saying, "Fuck off" and hang up. Someone anonymously tipped me off that the National Front had put my telephone number on display in most of the public conveniences in south London. Although my friends and family did not thank me for my abusive responses, eventually the offenders got fed up and moved on.

My first head-on clashes with a few representatives of the print media came soon after it was announced by the GLC that, following a process of open advertisement, applications and interviews, I was to be appointed to head up the new Ethnic Minorities Unit. I was still at Lambeth when I received a call from the local vicar, Ian, who lived a few doors from me in Peckham. He told me that a national newspaper journalist had knocked on his door asking if I was a communist, or one of Ken Livingstone's 'Reds under the bed'. At this point, I had never previously met Ken Livingstone. I also had journalists pushing their cameras through the letter box at home when they could get no other response. A reporter from one of the broadsheet national newspapers confronted me at County Hall during my first day and asked me if I was 'a left-winger'. Surprisingly, his published article the next day paraphrased my sarcastic reply in footballing terms. I had responded that, "I had two left feet but was a natural right-winger!"

The newly elected GLC had recruited a number of high-profile individuals, who were academically and professionally acclaimed for their understanding and experiences in the disciplines of strategic planning, social and cultural provision to meet different and special needs and economic development. They were appointed to lead on the new policies and programmes. Because there was an urgency to build trust and confidence across the capital city, the emphasis was to be on high tax and high spend investment in infrastructure, social provision and enterprise opportunities for people who were described as the "usually excluded".

The task of the Ethnic Minorities Unit was to reach out to all ethnic groups across London, encourage them to engage with the public institutions and organisations that serve society, collaborate with agencies working for justice and, through their own self-help initiatives, help the authorities in their quest to meet identified social and economic needs. A fundamental aim was to enable London's vulnerable communities to engage and become involved with democratic and local authority processes. This was about tackling discrimination and exclusion, building trust and confidence and letting them know that they mattered; that their contributions to London and the UK were valued and that they should strive to be socially and culturally active citizens with a focus on fairness for all. They were invited to utilise facilities at County Hall in pursuance of the equality of access objectives, and were assisted with some resources in the form of small grants to get their projects off the ground. They were able to access County Hall like never before to meet with elected councillors, attend consultations and events and secure help and guidance with job creation projects.

Newly formed committees of elected members covering the topics of industry and employment, women's equality, police monitoring and ethnic minorities were created and operated alongside previously established committees. This was the decision-making infrastructure to oversee a new dawn of public service provision in Greater London, which would endeavour to empower people to take some control of issues around them, get involved and contribute to bringing about better community relations, social cohesion, cultural expression and harmony. The vision was for London to evolve into and become the most vibrant and dynamic, multidimensional, multicultural, multilingual, multi-faith and multi-ethnic city in the world. This was in 1981, when few people could realistically have predicted what London would be like nearly four decades later: a magnet for visitors and settlers from all over the world.

The GLC, which was to last for only another four years, struggled to shed the media-inspired image that it was spendthrift, irresponsible and politically extreme. The leadership continuously clashed with government. However, the elected members were serious about creating jobs, defending vulnerable communities, investing in infrastructure, tackling inequalities and holding the other statutory undertakings in the city to account for performance and value for money. The council also offered views on national and international matters, which incensed the government and ultimately led to its abolition in 1985.

Throughout the GLC's early period from its creation in 1965, it had had little or no discernible interest in ethnic or race relations in London. During the period of the 1980s, ethnic minorities' concerns became relevant for consideration even though they were largely invisible among the decision making politicians. There was only one elected Black councillor from the 1980 elections, Paul Boateng, who was a vocal and highly effective elected member of the new GLC, someone ethnic minorities could identify as 'one of our own'. Paul was chair of the Police Monitoring Committee and was pivotal in pushing his colleagues on all issues of inequality and exclusion and giving prominence to ethnic minority needs and participation in decision-making. Although his priority was with this committee, he often intervened, appropriately and objectively, in others where they were seen to overlook equality considerations and were continuing to operate with discriminatory processes and incomplete decision-making. Whenever asked, he was an enthusiastic and willing participant and vocal presence everywhere within London's diverse communities, and yet had a young family to whom he was devoted. He was also a practising solicitor and was often rushing from court into committee and council meetings. There is one special endearing and typically genuine image of Paul during that period that remains so vivid in my memory bank. It was witnessing him arriving at County Hall directly from a session at court with a bundle of papers in one hand and his baby daughter held safely with the other, and rushing into a committee to ask for an item to be reconsidered in order to ensure that equality considerations were factored into the decisions they were making. It was no surprise that he went on to serve with distinction as a Member of Parliament, ultimately serving the nation in government as a cabinet member and, later, as a diplomat with high commissioner status and now a member of the House of Lords.

At the beginning of the 1980s, there was a focus on why ethnic minority communities were invisible when it came to the uniformed public services – the police, ambulance and fire services. The GLC was responsible for the London Fire Service and members wanted to know why there was only a handful of Black or Asian firefighters, and no women. The management's glib responses were that applications *were* received from ethnic minorities but Asian applicants were successful in passing the written test but did not have the lung capacity to pass the physical test; and the African/ Caribbean applicants could pass the physical tests but failed the written ones. When challenged to explain who put the fires out in Asian and African countries, no answer was forthcoming. Their response to the lack of women in the service was derisory, including, "They are not interested; do not have the same strength as men; not suitable for sliding down poles; no female toilet facilities," etc.

Members of the Fire Service management team then went to the United States to see and learn how minorities and women became not only active firefighters but were often managing and running the services. On their return, they expressed realisation that change was now essential. Those who were not committed to the essential changes were encouraged to move on. Nepotism and discrimination would end and open recruitment, training and staff development would be priorities. Positive action advertising was introduced, using actors to illustrate images of Black, Asian and women firefighters. These were placed in national and local newspapers. Career officers were appointed to encourage applications, which duly arrived.

All resistance, reluctance and apprehension from management and trade unions were quickly brushed aside by members determined to have a fire service that reflected the changing demographic profile of London. These open access and equality measures resulted in a high-quality intake of new recruits from all sections of society, including those who would not previously have applied because they did not know how to do so, saw no images of themselves and felt unwelcome. After the new processes were implemented, monitoring evidence showed that, year on year, the intake of recruits and trainees was of a high standard with all entrants going through the most rigorous tests before appointment. Thus emerged a new and more inclusive London Fire Service that began to reflect the communities it served, and included Black, Asian and women firefighters.

As with all organisational and institutional reforms, there are conflicts and casualties. Whenever new initiatives yielded results planned for, there was a tendency to regard the success as easy wins. The equality gains from 1981 to 1984 were never easily achieved. Virtually every proposed change was criticised, opposed, and countered, with good as well as specious arguments. Traditional established practices were underpinned by a dominant culture of 'we have always done it our way successfully'. Those themes of resistance to change and political opposition, negative media coverage, government and legal challenges were all factors that constrained the implementation of justifiable and much needed positive action programmes. It was a never-ending path of attrition, motivated by a desire to frustrate the administration until, sooner or later, they would abandon these equality initiatives and move on to the next set of trendy priorities.

The area of public procurement was a major activity of the GLC. It also had a huge supplies operation for all inner London schools, colleges and many other public service bodies. The GLC announced in 1981 that it wanted all of its 40,000 plus contractors and suppliers on its approved list to comply with equality legislation, and that it intended to incorporate this requirement into all contracts. Contractors and suppliers were asked to provide data and information about their equality policies as part of the standard process of getting onto the council's approved list.

There was a huge national outcry. The Confederation of Business Industry (CBI) and central government led the charge of hell-fire and fury, loaded with threats of legal challenges coming from different sections of the business community and trade associations. A key concession, that enabled the equality contract compliance project to succeed, was that each contractor and supplier was given the right to remain on the approved list if they were prepared to become compliant. Thus, suppliers were not simply excluded if they had no effective equality policies or declared commitments; the choice remained with them and the GLC offered to assist each with the equality compliance process, should they wish to access such help. If they wanted the GLC's business, they had to compete for it and, if they wanted to be on the approved list of contractors and suppliers, they would have to meet the standard conditions set by the council, all of which was deemed to be reasonable and lawful. End of story. The vast majority were prepared to meet all the requirements with very few deciding to go their own way. However, the fact that most agreed to stay on the approved list and to be in compliance did not mean that they vigorously pursued equality and fair policies and practices. For some it was tokenism, for others it was a recognition that equality and fairness was something to take note of and even make it happen, albeit on a slow basis.

But, it was a pivotal moment not to have backed off, and to exercise reasonableness and pragmatism in paving the way for ultimate success in making policies and processes fairer and getting more people eventually to see the business benefits for all.

Other areas of progressive activity included the arts, leisure and recreational services. The chair of the Arts Committee then was Tony Banks, an ebullient character who went on to become a prominent Member of Parliament. While at the GLC, he was up-front in challenging arts and film bodies to end the discrimination and the marginalisation of Black, Asian and other minority ethnic artists, performers, managers and technicians. They had restricted access to opportunities and that had to change for the GLC to continue with its support. The GLC then introduced its own programme of support for the community led arts projects. Provision was made to provide grants and investment in minority arts, film-making, new creative arts and professional development. It was to contribute to a growing infrastructure which would form a strong base for the development of the multi-talented, multicultural arts and culture sector we see flourishing today in London, something that is admired by visitors to the UK from all over the world.

The GLC also attracted considerable unreasonable media criticism of its outreach work that connected with women's and LGBTQ organisations. Fortunately, the media was more generous in its praise for the much-needed progressive initiatives for disabled people, particularly in relation to transport needs and accessible provision.

Among the many minority ethnic communities that articulated their agenda for equality and fair treatment were the Irish community in London. Many of the elected members shared some Irish heritage, and some were very upfront in voicing their support for such causes, including the Leader, Ken Livingstone, and the Deputy Leader, John McDonnell. They were not slow in aligning themselves to the struggles in Ireland. This, however, did not deflect from their understanding of the reality of discrimination against Irish people in London. After all, it was not too long ago that blatant public race discrimination with explicit notices saying, 'no Blacks, no Coloureds, no Irish, no dogs' had been made unlawful. The Irish in Britain organisation, particularly those based in the London Borough of Brent, were strident in their demands for education that reflected their history, culture and struggles, a recognition of their contribution to the economy, particularly in construction, and the importance of being recognised as a minority ethnic community entitled to protection from race discrimination under the scope of the Race Relations Act 1976.

The GLC also prioritised action to assist Traveller, Gypsy and Roma communities, who were regarded as the most discriminated against and excluded group of people. Local authorities had a responsibility to provide adequate sites for encampments but, as there were very few official sites, many unlawful encampments were created and this caused conflict with local residents and businesses. The GLC's aim, working with local councils, was to oversee and increase the number of sites and provide essential facilities such as running water, sanitary provision and access to electricity.

On one occasion, I visited the Westway's Traveller site, located under the flyover on the A40 between White City and Shepherd's Bush in west London. The purpose of my visit was to ascertain what particular needs the community had. Even though the residents on site were informed of the date and time of my arrival, they were very distrustful of outsiders, especially those in suits or police uniforms. I was greeted by dogs barking, open fires and suspicious looks. The site, I was assured, was self-managed and the needs were exactly those we had identified – electricity, running water and basic health facilities. They also wanted to be free from media and police harassment. The struggles of Traveller, Gypsy and Roma people to be treated fairly and with dignity and respect, to live their lives within their culture and to be given space to interact with local services, facilities and resources continue today. Campaigning groups are working tirelessly to secure meaningful responses from government at all levels to address more appropriately the race discrimination these communities continue to face, as evidenced in the government's own Race Disparities Audit, revealed in 2017. That struggle goes on.

In a world so riddled with inequalities, the GLC faced many competing demands for attention with all manner of mainstream and extreme politics lobbying for their claims for support to be addressed. No-one was reaching for the stars; they merely wanted a fairer share. However, essentially, there was a struggle between the GLC and the government. The council wanted to use its financial base to tackle social and economic disadvantage and the government wanted to restrict its spending capacity and thwart its ambitions. London was politically polarised. The government and its flagship Conservative controlled councils opposed the high spending GLC and its ambitions to redress the equality imbalance by redirecting resources to wherever it considered was most in need. One such area was housing.

In the early 1980s, as today, there was considerable pressure for the provision of housing to meet the needs of newly settled ethnic minority communities as well as other pressing needs of families in deprived localities. Post-war immigration had induced the concept of 'white flight' with white households moving away from areas of Black or Asian settlement in search of what they considered to be better quality housing and schools for their children. Racial prejudice also would have fed the desire of some of those wanting to move away. Council owned accommodation, particularly of the worst quality and in older estates in relatively poor and deprived boroughs like Tower Hamlets, became the homes for Bangladeshi families. This, in consequence, led to acute racial harassment, extreme hate activities and meant that families lived in fear. Wherever there were concentrated communities, such as Thamesmead and East London, Asian, Black and minority ethnic communities had to organise resistance to defend against extreme racist and fascist attacks and harassment. The GLC was very sympathetic in offering assistance to all such vulnerable communities.

As well as being the strategic regional housing authority tasked with the provision of priority accommodation, the GLC was also responsible for investing in and providing resources for back-up advisory and family support services, as well as for community solidarity in building resistance against racism and discrimination. Grants through the Ethnic Minorities Committee were awarded to local self-help organisations, particularly to assist with language, translation and interpretation activities, training and education for employment and in dealing with the authorities. Inevitably, there was both political and media opposition to the grants being awarded by the Ethnic Minorities Committee. Very early in the cycle of meetings, the Conservative opposition made it clear that they would be opposing many of the recommendations for grants to minority ethnic groups. At one particular meeting, there were over fifty applications for projects for approval. The meeting was formally convened in the appropriate way, all the Labour members arrived on time, but the Conservatives were still in their group meeting plotting how to thwart any grants being approved. They arrived three minutes late and found that every item had been properly approved as observed by the committee clerks and legal officer. They were never, ever late again for another Committee meeting.

The competition for grants was intense, and organisations would find ways to criticise the council if they were not benefitting from allocation decisions and would often go out of their way to demonstrate bias.

One prominent local campaigner, Mr Haque, attended most, if not all of the grant-making committees, and wrote extensively to all and sundry about bias against the Bangladeshi community. He claimed that they were the victims of discrimination and inequality in grant allocation. His letters were eloquently written, with sound arguments although not always backed up by evidence. After about eighteen months of battering on doors which were ajar but not opening fully, his style and approach became more menacing and persistent. He attended meetings and events with a camera and took photographs throughout. His intention, he said, was to expose, "bent and corrupt decision-makers," but months later, it was suggested that his threats might have little substance because the camera probably had no film in it. In the end, perhaps, he felt a sense of achievement when the government turned its ire on the GLC and brought forward legislation in 1985 to abolish it.

The GLC was an easy target for criticism and attack, but it did set the scene for bold and progressive policies to make London a vibrant, inclusive and dynamic multicultural capital city. No surprise, therefore, when in 2000, the Blair New Labour government reintroduced independent government for London with the establishment of the Greater London Authority, to be run by an elected mayor. No surprise, either, that Greater London electors voted for Ken Livingstone as its first mayor. Having fallen out of favour with his beloved Labour Party, he stood as an independent, and triumphed.

SEVEN

Back to the future

By 1984, after three years of intense strife and stress as well as many successful innovations and initiatives, I decided that it was time for a change from the GLC environment. This took me back to Lambeth, where I was appointed as assistant chief executive. Before making the move I attended a celebratory event which was organised by the GLC to launch the designation of London as leading a campaign under the banner of 'London Against Racism'. Attracting the iconic music superstar, Stevie Wonder, to County Hall to launch the event was particularly stunning, as he is a truly magnificent internationally renowned humanitarian, who cares about justice, human rights and equality for all. There may not have been universal support for the initiative but, for many, clearly it was easier to be against racism than to eliminate it. The fundamental purpose of the project was to raise public awareness of the GLC's serious intent to pursue policies and programmes to minimise the adverse impact of racism and all forms of discrimination. It was also seeking to do so with the support from, and involvement of, all ethnic groups of people in London.

On my return to the staff of Lambeth Borough Council, it was soon apparent that the council was still engulfed in a struggle with the government. The council had its rate support grant limits set by government below the council's expectations, so it was difficult for it to approve balanced budgets because its proposed expenditure would always

Pictured with Stevie Wonder at the launch of the GLC's London
Against Racism campaign at Lambeth South Bank in January 1984.

exceed its expected income. The council failed to collect all
of the domestic rates levied because many households could
not afford to pay, and the council refused to make cuts,
wanting to fulfil implementation of its planned services. At
one stage, because the council had failed to set a legal
budget, early morning meetings had to be held involving
leading members and chief officers to decide on what
expenditure could be incurred lawfully to ensure that
essential statutory services such as children in care, public
health and safety and critical housing maintenance were
delivered. As a consequence, discretionary services suffered.

My specific role as assistant chief executive was to bring
coherence to a range of policy initiatives, including all the
equality programmes, and develop and implement a
Community Involvement and Participation Strategy in line
with the council's commitment to devolve powers and

resources to local neighbourhood communities. It was a potentially exciting and attractive project. Community development was a big feature across the borough but it had developed randomly with elected members having their own 'pet projects' that served their wards and constituencies. Councillors were always under pressure to back their local supporters or face the consequences at the ballot box. The work on equalities continued but the coherent strategy envisaged for it within the Community Involvement and Participation Project stalled, and many local neighbourhood and borough-wide organisations struggled to make ends meet and respond to increasing demands from local residents.

The dynamic Councillor Linda Bellos, for a period the leader of the council, was an equalities champion in the finest sense of the term. She played a very significant role in challenging resistance to change and scrutinising the equalities initiatives enthusiastically and effectively. There was competition for attention and resources between the Race Relations Unit, the Women's Unit, the Disability Discrimination Unit, the grants unit and so on. Everyone, not unreasonably, regarded their respective area of activity as more deserving of additional resources than the rest, and each worked tirelessly to enlist community support and sympathetic councillors to lobby on their behalf.

There was a siege mentality of 'them and us' most of the time, which made it difficult to get people to come together and work collectively for the benefit of the most needy residents in the borough. It would be fair to say that each person involved was, more often than not, seriously and sincerely dedicated to supporting equality and human rights commitments, but also fought for the particular interests they represented. Local people, in the main, appeared to be in sympathy with the council's struggle with government to obtain adequate resources and, whilst also understanding the government's responsibility to distribute resources fairly across the whole country, generally felt that

With Walter Sisulu, senior ANC anti apartheid campaigner in
1986 during a tour of community development and housing
projects in the London Borough of Lambeth

the government was not being fair or non-partisan when it
came to the allocation of resources for deprived and
disadvantaged communities.

In the end the council would have no choice but to
approve a lawful balanced budget in order to function on a
daily basis and meet its statutory obligations. The
reluctantly agreed budget, inevitably, fell short of being
adequate to meet many of the identified needs. There was
substantial evidence of serious deprivation, with apparent
community frustration at the failure to meet such needs
more effectively, and the likelihood of impending battles
between the police and some sections of the local community.
Councillors were challenged in the courts, surcharged and
disqualified for not acting lawfully, all the while claiming
the moral high ground for defending poor communities in
the borough and pointing to unmet needs which were

disadvantaging many residents. The 'them and us' experience became debilitating. Highly charged meetings with politicians, council officers and community interest groups often took the administration down cul-de-sacs with promises being broken and needs left unmet. There was dismay among local activists and equality campaigners who held the views that genuine local decision-making, with devolved responsibilities and resources, would not happen along the lines envisaged and hoped for. As a result, rather than coming together as we had hoped, many organisations were now in self-help, self-interest and self-defence modes.

On reflection, the prime minister of the day, Margaret Thatcher, who, with many of her followers, promoted individualism and did not appear to believe in the concept of society, had the upper-hand. In such situations, central government virtually always wins confrontations with local government. "Everybody for themselves", and "stand on your own two feet", were central features of the PM's mantra! She never hesitated in being forthright as the country's leader about any matter in which she held strident views. She was upfront, unhesitant in immediately branding the young people who were involved in violent battles with the police during the 1985 disturbances as 'criminals', despite the genuine local grievances that existed. Of course, most local people regretted and condemned the violence, rioting and lawlessness that led to extensive damage to property and the breakdown of trust and confidence. But some of the young people, who had marginalised existences on the streets, did not see themselves as having access to improved quality of life opportunities. They felt no obligation to the mainstream option of being compliant with a scenario in which their daily reality was having to face those charged with keeping the peace and keeping them in their place in a corrupt, unequal society. The prime minister, however, was not for changing. She supported the police 100 per cent, so nothing was altered.

At that time and in such neighbourhoods, too many people were living in demoralised environments, with a lack of optimism, trust and confidence. The outlook was bleak for some people as they saw it. The local political priorities were skewed. The toxic environment of conflict and confrontation made it difficult to make progress with the community and participation strategy. Community groups, with their own particular interests, were losing patience with the council to deliver the resources to meet local needs. Obviously, such failure was a collective one. Councillors, executives and advisers were equally regarded as culpable. For me, it was a sad loss of personal and professional credibility. No matter how much I felt that I and others were doing to engage positively with local community organisations, there was a sense of impotency due to our failure to meet the expectations and obligations. I needed to move on, to find a new horizon, a new challenge. Radical change, as hoped for in Lambeth, was not likely to be effected in such a febrile environment of fear, distrust, deception and dashed hopes.

EIGHT

A new focus; a new challenge

The new challenge came in 1986 with the opportunity to pitch my experiences, management and leadership qualities in the field of education as director of education (equalities) with the Inner London Education Authority (ILEA). The ILEA was an independent body but also a statutory committee of the soon-to-be defunct GLC. As it was to become a stand-alone local education authority, it wanted to give new and coherent leadership on equality matters. On arrival, I was reminded of my first week at the GLC as the head of its new Ethnic Minorities Unit in 1981.

When I took up that post at the GLC, I was overwhelmed initially by letters of complaint about racial discrimination in the ILEA from Black, Asian and other minority ethnic teachers and inspectors. It was an astonishing batch of heart-breaking accounts on an unimaginable scale. It included allegations of harassment, being overlooked for promotion, demotions, grievances denied and ruthless disciplinary processes to keep people from progressing. Many of the complainants also focused on the failure of the education system to meet the educational needs of Black and white working-class boys, disproportionate exclusions and the classification of Black boys as 'educationally sub-normal' (ESN). Many of these were historic complaints but many more were part of the daily experiences of Black and Asian employees in the London education system. Complainants hoped that, somehow, I would be able to help them as a result of my newly acquired status as an adviser in the GLC. However, during my first week at the GLC I had been told in no uncertain terms by the hierarchy's management, led by Director General Sir James Swaffield, that I was a GLC employee, the ILEA was a separate organisation and I was not to get involved in ILEA matters. Put bluntly, I might as well put the complaints in the bin, which in effect is what happened. Once again my credibility took an instant knock, as many of the complainants either saw my role as one of tokenism or believed that I had failed to use my 'non-existent power' to help them with their grievances.

There was suspicion in my mind at the time, reinforced by views expressed to me by some of the discontented, that the then ILEA boss, Sir Peter Newsam, had leaned on the GLC and insisted that I kept my nose out of their business. Interestingly, later that year, Sir Peter Newsam left the ILEA when he was appointed chair of the Commission for Racial Equality. Now, as I joined the ILEA some five years after joining the GLC and having to back away from issues in the ILEA, many of the same aggrieved individuals were still around, hoping that justice and fairness would at last become a reality following my arrival. It seemed to me that history was about to repeat itself, yet again, with high expectations for me to resolve their historic and ongoing grievances.

The ILEA was regarded as the largest education authority in Western Europe, and provided education services from cradle to grave across the twelve inner London boroughs and the City of London. It also offered further education, including specialist colleges, such as furniture craft, and higher education provision through the network of polytechnics prior to their re-designation as universities. Adult education institutes offered day-time and day care provision, evening classes, leisure facilities and training. There was careers education and a careers service in each inner London borough catchment area with specialist and expert back-up services, and a high-quality inspectorate led by a highly respected chief inspector.

I had been surprised and delighted to be offered the ILEA post but had to think long and hard about whether I really wanted the job. Firstly, it was a huge task with vast expectations of what must be achieved. Further, the Chief Education Officer, Sir William Stubbs, had made it clear to me that, while he had no doubt about my ability to do the job (we had previously worked together on a city challenge education project for adolescents in Lambeth), there would be resentment from 'education professionals' because I had no direct experience as a teacher or lecturer. I reminded him that it was a management rather than a teaching or lecturing position and there was no basis on which to question my credentials. There were other significant doubts too: trust and confidence. Sir William sought my assurance that, as a member of the senior management team, I would respect the confidentiality of all discussions and decision-making. I had no hesitation in giving him the assurance he sought, but I made it clear that if I found anything that, in my view, worked against equality, it would if necessary be referred elsewhere to get a resolution and fair outcome. This was my stance from the outset, making it clear that I was not prepared to be a 'yes man', nor keep my head down and not challenge the organisational culture or resistance to change. I understood the reality – that there would be obstacles to overcome. There would be specialist and exclusive networks. If there was anything they did not want me to know, they would not tell me. They would have their own private meetings and discussions on matters from which I would be excluded if they felt I was a threat to them. So, being defiant and up for the challenge, the guy from Peckham said, "Yes, let's give it a go." It was a very difficult decision. Survival was back on my personal and professional agendas and my stamina, instincts, experiences, skills and personal qualities now had to be at their sharpest and most convincing.

Luckily for me, in taking on this new assignment I found that there were many people on-side who supported the strong and comprehensive equality policies and wanted to provide the necessary back-up to secure their implementation. Among the elected members were individuals such as the formidable leader, Frances Morrell, who did not suffer fools gladly, and her deputy, Bernard Wiltshire. He was bold, brash and unequivocal in his demands that equality and quality were prioritised in the education of all children and students. He was also clear on what a multicultural curriculum should look like and how it should benefit all those from multi-ethnic and multilingual backgrounds. Others, including Lorna Boreland-Kelly, former ILEA staff from multi-ethnic backgrounds, community educators and enlightened current senior staff, were all keen to contribute to the ILEA's equality and quality education programme and its implementation across the entirety of the service.

The government at the time, especially the Secretary of State for Education, Kenneth Baker, was never enthusiastic about the ILEA. Both he and the government disapproved of its emphasis on high expenditure and its commitment to an accessible, multicultural curriculum taught by highly skilled teachers, despite the fact that it enabled under-achievers from all backgrounds to learn and be inspired by its range and content. The ILEA was confident that its education offer was of high quality, and the records of achievements for each child were testimony to how its schools were contributing to raising educational standards and achieving good results.

From an equality in education perspective, there were many problems to be acknowledged and to confront and resolve. The renowned Research and Statistics department, led by the dynamic Peter Mortimore, was never slow in bringing forward evidence to illustrate trends, successes, failures and achievements. This consistently demonstrated the under-achievement of Black boys and some Asian groups, as well as high achievement among other minority ethnic children such as those of Chinese and Indian heritage. It also did not shy away from highlighting underachievement of white children from disadvantaged backgrounds and from inadequate and unequal opportunities. Suspensions and exclusions disproportionately impacted on Black children, and there was a considerable amount of alleged race and sex discrimination against Black and Asian teachers and inspectors as well as those in other positions.

Squaring the circle of education inequalities inevitably proved difficult. It was always easier to talk about aims and aspirations and provide evidence of the negatives. But transforming education and delivering equality required a long-term investment in high quality teachers from all ethnic backgrounds, support for families in disadvantaged households and additional pre-school and after-school provision for children with special and particular needs. It also meant raising the aspirations of children from disadvantaged backgrounds, refocusing the curriculum to give due recognition to the relevance and importance of different faiths and cultures and ensuring that the principles of equality and fair treatment permeated the entire service.

Black parents were increasingly vociferous about the impact of the education system on many of their boys, who were often branded 'educationally sub-normal' for little or no other reason than racism. The failure of the education providers, schools and teaching staff led to demands for alternative provision, such as independent Saturday and Sunday schools, run by Black teachers. Many of these had already been set up on a voluntary basis across London and other parts of the country to provide those children being denied a full and adequate education with supplementary and, in some cases, their basic education. Complaints often focused on the low expectations that some schools and teachers held for their Black pupils, especially the boys. Some progress was made over the ensuing decades in trying to tackle this deficiency in education provision. However, in 2021, it still rankles because of school exclusion policies and social and economic disadvantages which disproportionately impact adversely on Black boys.

During my time at the ILEA I had no doubt that most of the elected members and many of their enlightened senior staff were committed to working to achieve the equality and quality outcomes for all pupils and students, as well as for staff and their performance. However, the polarised politics of state-provided education had become a controversial and toxic topic in London. By 1988, the government had decided it would no longer allow the ILEA to pursue its explicit educational goals and Parliament was persuaded to abolish the Authority. It was to be replaced with new, individually-run local education authorities in each of the twelve London boroughs and the City of London.

The political battle to save the ILEA was ultimately unsuccessful, but such conflicts often end in tears given that government holds the whip hand. The ILEA had to restructure itself to respond meaningfully to the 'Great Education Reforms' proposed by the government. The Chief Education Officer, William Stubbs, left to head the new Higher Education Funding Council to oversee the transformation of polytechnics into fully fledged universities. Frances Morrell was replaced as Leader of the ILEA by Neil Fletcher, who previously had oversight of the Authority's highly acclaimed further and higher education provision. A new structure was created for the final two years of the authority with David Mallen becoming its chief education officer, while I was successful somehow in being appointed to the position of chief executive. With the political battle over, it was time to focus on how to transfer services, facilities and resources as seamlessly as practicable to ensure that each new education authority would be to function effectively from day one in April 1990.

Co-ordinating and planning for the transfer was the responsibility of Peter Howlett, a first-class administrator and manager with a sharp eye for detail and a determination to see any project through from beginning to end. Committees, working parties, consultations, shadow authorities and liaison officers in each borough emerged to energise the game-changing processes that would lead to the new LEAs for education provision in inner London, which would be similar to what already existed in the other twenty outer London boroughs.

The most heart-breaking aspect of this upheaval was its impact on staff who had emotional and professional affections for educating Londoners that dated back to the days of the former London County Council (LCC). Many long-serving staff opposed the ILEA's abolition and volunteered for early retirement or redundancy, while others became new recruits for the putative LEAs and signed up to assist with preparations for hand-over day and a seamless transition. There was an overall feeling among many that they were doing the government's dirty work in destroying much of the excellence achieved over decades by the LCC and the ILEA. In reality, however, we needed to fulfil our obligations as public servants and do so as effectively as possible. That there were so few failings to report in April 1990, when the new authorities became functional, was a tribute to all those involved in undertaking this massive reform in line with the wishes of Parliament and the government, irrespective of individual personal and professional views.

NINE

Unfinished business

As one door closed, I looked for another to open so that I could get back on the public service career trail. In the dying days of the ILEA I felt that, as chief executive, I had an obligation to be there to support colleagues who were in the front line of change whilst still delivering day-to-day services. Abolition date was 31st March 1990, and during that final month I decided to put my name in the frame for the vacant post of chief executive of Lambeth Council. This post would not have been my first choice (if there was a choice to be made), but I needed to work, and wanted to get going straight away. I felt that I had unfinished business there and should not shy away from the challenge. So, I was duly appointed to what many people told me was an impossible job and a veritable 'poisoned chalice'. The print media also described it as the most difficult job in local government. Some even said it was impossible to do. No pressure then!

In retrospect, it would become clear that I carelessly underestimated the depth of the problems I would have to face. Conflict was generated by some councillors who were hell-bent on fulfilling what they considered to be their obligations to constituents, supporters and disadvantaged communities that required more and better access to public services. The previous incumbent as chief executive, John George, was very amiable and functional in his approach. He was not only chief executive but also at times the chief solicitor. There was an existing culture in the hierarchy where the senior politicians owned the chief officers. In that context the chief executive did what the politicians wanted and what he knew would be necessary to keep them sweet. But he carefully sidestepped some of the thorniest realities of the day-to-day management by his chief officer colleagues, who operated within their own, self-contained fiefdoms. This had the effect of enabling incredible and impenetrable relationships to be built up between chief officers and their respective elected chairs. Such arrangements are obviously essential in local authorities to ensure effective and efficient operations. However, in Lambeth it was more about departmental protectionism, holding onto existing resources while pleading for more, withholding information or data which would reveal under-performance or failure. Their powerful positions also enabled them to discreetly marginalise corporate-led initiatives such as the council's equalities policies and programmes.

At the top of my agenda was the budget. The council had not been collecting the Poll Tax and finances were extremely underwhelming compared to planned expenditure. The management structure needed reform, processes required streamlining and modernising, over three thousand posts would have to be removed from the payroll and that was just for starters. The hierarchical mould had to be broken to create a dynamic corporate management team to take forward the council's initiatives. Several options to merge different directorates were proposed. We also had to sacrifice around four or five heads of directorates as part of the personnel cull in pursuit of a lawful balanced budget.

Inevitably, I was the seen as the 'executioner' required to deliver the suggested savings, making enemies, being screamed at by the trade unions and staff associations but having to press ahead with these essential changes. It was never going to be a party in the park but, at times, the abuse was withering and demoralising. However, leading politicians remained supportive, for which I was grateful, and opposition councillors were mostly professional in their criticism of the executive, reserving their venom for political foes.

What I did not see coming was the ruling Labour-led administration fracturing into several different factions. This was precipitated by the then leader of the national Labour Party, Neil Kinnock and his executive council. They suspended thirteen Lambeth Labour councillors, thus removing the party whip and their control of the council. All of a sudden I was vulnerable. As an example, on one occasion, I had meticulously prepared yet another paper on further transforming service delivery arrangements and staffing reforms for which opposition councillors expressed support. One prominent elected member among the opposition leaders overenthusiastically and calculatingly went on to say that they had been waiting for many years for such far-reaching proposals. On hearing this, some members from the ruling party, who had given my proposals their cautious prior blessing and had committed to support in a committee vote, declared: "If you are supporting it we will oppose!" The situation had become almost unmanageable.

At the same time, I was being bombarded by individual residents who saw me as a short circuit route to solving long-standing problems with the council. On one very frightening occasion, I arrived back after a lunch break to find three huge local guys sitting in my office. I was surprised, but tried to hide the fear engulfing me as I desperately tried to put up an appearance of not being intimidated. They told me that I had 10 days to sort out their long-standing housing problems with the council. My immediate reaction was, "Or what? What would you do after ten days? Kill me? Then you really will have problems and I will have none!" They seemed to be stunned by my bullishness and went on to be a bit more reasonable in articulating their frustrations and demands. They told me that they had come to me because local people had told them that I was approachable and "a good guy." No pressure! Some matters took longer than others and the rest were impossible. Their concerns were re-routed to the appropriate directorate and personnel. Happily, I never had to deal direct with those guys again, but nor am I able to say whether their problems were finally resolved. Perhaps, because they did not come back to me, they achieved satisfactory outcomes. On the other hand, they may have concluded that I was also a waste of space!

One of the biggest challenges which emerged, as another bolt out of the blue, concerned direct labour activities. Known as Direct Labour Organisations (DLOs), these were operations packaged as discrete 'organisations' undertaking as independent contractors on behalf of the client, the appropriate council department. DLOs were set up by the council and operated on a profit-making basis with budgets and accounts audited and signed off by the district auditor in compliance with legal requirements. There was some scepticism about the DLOs and their efficiency, but no obvious reason or basis upon which to be concerned about their management and operational competency, other than the ongoing allegations that they were not efficient in commercial terms.

However, it was drawn to my attention that consistent annual profits were being made by the DLO for street and highway maintenance yet there were ongoing complaints from the public about pot-holes in the roads in several parts of the borough. That was the simple version of the issue, but these areas are full of complexity. The department responsible said it had completed tens of thousands of repair jobs, especially pot-hole repairs, but initial enquiries indicated some difficulty to verify with absolute clarity who placed the orders for repairs, who did the work, where and when it was undertaken and inspected, and who drew up the invoices and authorised the payments. Members agreed that this situation warranted an urgent investigation into 'corrupt practices.'

I immediately put together a team of four chief officers to work with me on this review. Almost everything we uncovered in our search to find evidence of these alleged 'corrupt' practices seemed mysteriously to vanish without trace. I also found it difficult to understand how a journalist on the local newspaper, the *South London Press*, was able to telephone me immediately after the weekly meetings of the investigating group and ask me questions to which he already had answers. Unknown to me at the time, my office was bugged. I became suspicious of each of the officers on my team but, without any tangible evidence of them working against me individually and collectively, still felt I had to trust them. One day, when I realised that two directors, both with a DLO in their department, were having secret briefings, I challenged them but their responses were unsatisfactory. I went to the Leader of the Council, Steve Whaley, and told him of my serious concerns and my immediate intention to dismiss one of the directors for incompetence in the way he ran his department and because he was untrustworthy. He was sympathetic but was not sure that I would get support from the key politicians for my proposal because of the compromised relations that certain chief officers had with leading politicians in the council. This proved to be the case. On returning to my office the director's chair was on the phone to tell me that there was no way he would let anyone get rid of his director and I had better back off now! That is the mild version of what I was actually told. To some extent I was already paralysed by the relationships between directors and their chairs because those protective bonds were used to resist change when it suited their personal and political interests rather than the interests of the council as a whole and the residents of the borough. Without the backing of the leader of the council and the chair of committee, my position of authority was severely compromised and I now knew the limits of my powers, notwithstanding my responsibilities. So I had to persist, in some ways as a partial lame duck, or walk away.

I was also the council's designated monitoring officer and, as such, was required to report any potential or actual unlawful activity formally to the policy committee and the council and send a copy of my Monitoring Report to the secretary of state for local government. Not surprisingly, the DLO story was leaked and appeared in a Sunday newspaper. The secretary of state was incensed that he had not been informed and I was summoned to meet him the following day, as were our director of finance and the district auditor. On arrival, the permanent secretary informed me that the minister was fuming over my failure to send him a copy of the Monitoring Report. At that point I reached into my pocket and handed him a piece of paper which he looked at with curiosity. No, it was not my letter of resignation or a grovelling apology. It was a delivery note which showed that the document had been delivered by hand to the department for the secretary of state and had been signed for as received. I was promptly told that I was no longer needed at the meeting and left the district auditor and the permanent secretary to deal with their own respective embarrassment.

I had now reached a point where I could no longer keep trying to manage change, deliver on equalities and continue to run the investigation into alleged mal-administration or even 'corruption' as it was impossible to gather any evidence that would enable me to identify failings and apportion blame. A few councillors insisted that I should keep going and name those they felt were responsible – they knew who they wanted to scapegoat. This I refused to do. I found myself stranded in several cul-de-sacs, facing blockages that prevented me from running the organisation in the most effective and professional way. I told the leader that I would not be seeking to extend my contract when my three-year term expired in the next seven months, in March 1993. He was not happy with this and told me that if I resigned, he would also have to go. However, my mind was made up. I was surrounded by people who were untrustworthy but impossible to nail because they were clever and cunning, and effective at covering their backs and those of their colleagues.

During the time of the investigation I had my car tyres slashed on several occasions, my windscreen was smashed and I received threatening phone calls. It was incredibly difficult to get up each morning knowing that I would have to face various stressful scenarios during the day. The day I told the leader I was leaving, even with no job to move onto, I started to feel a lot better. I was a new person as I experienced the weight of responsibility and all the stress evaporating. I was still up for the challenge but now I could tell it like it was. I wanted to show my contempt for those who deserved my wrath and did so because there was nothing to be gained from being honourable or dignified in dealing with such colleagues. During my final months, the leader tried to persuade me to stay with the possibility of a four-year contract and better terms but, for me, my local government days were almost at an end.

Sadly, it had proved mission impossible for me and to stay would have been wrong for both me and the council. I really had to go. I also had to leave behind some unfinished business that I had hoped to complete when I took on the assignment in 1990. During my stint there, many things were achieved by well-led senior managers and their competent and committed staff. All of that happened in spite of an environment riven with chaotic oversight at chief officer and political level. Although, because of all the diversions, undermining and many allegations of corrupt practice and failures, I was not able to provide the level of support and guidance to some of the chief officers and key staff that, in retrospect, I should and would have offered. Nevertheless, I know that I had succeeded in putting in place some of the essential stepping stones and processes needed to reform the executive management structure and help the council to move forward with essential changes. Those, at least, would enable my successors to progress quickly with their efforts to take the council forward under any newly elected administration.

It was somewhat of a relief to me and my sanity that my successors, over the ensuing months, managed to shift the directors that I was prevented from dismissing. In doing so, they were able to unearth the evidence of corrupt networks, one of which was dedicated to marginalise and undermine my efforts to reform the management structures of the council and to thwart my investigations into corruption. Not surprisingly, there were expressions of shock when it was also revealed in the *London Evening Standard* that my office and home telephones had been bugged by at least one of the chief officers, in collusion with others, for a period during my term in office. It appeared that some people could not bring themselves to believe that such activities would have been possible in local government in the 1990s. It was clear and hurtful to me to understand the reality that no other chief executive in any other local authority could have been bugged and undermined to such an extent by subordinates, who were allowed to get away with it. The powerful secretive networks of staff and members were thankfully dismantled after I had gone.

My departure meant that my nightmare was over. Phew! But, the struggle for many local residents would go on for much longer. My love affair with Lambeth Council was finally at an end and I was on the lookout for another job. For some, the verdict was that I tried to go too far too fast; for others I should have been more radical. For me, it was a hell of an experience that tested my resilience and my personal and professional commitment to the effective, efficient and appropriate public services provision.

TEN

Defying the odds and doing more with less

When I told friends and trusted colleagues it had been suggested that I apply for the soon-to-be vacant post of Chair of the Commission for Racial Equality (CRE) they thought I had some sort of death wish. Having seen me move from Lambeth to the GLC, back to Lambeth, then to the ILEA and yet again back to Lambeth, the CRE was seen not as a case of out of the frying pan into the fire but heading straight into an erupting volcano. I did not see it quite that way and, facing the prospect of being out of work, testing myself in competition for a job on a national scale aroused my instincts for a new challenge. In those days it was quite unusual for such positions to be advertised as they were usually in the gift of the home secretary. On this occasion, however, it was to be an open competition with interviews by civil servants and then the home secretary. Ahh... equal opportunities at work, apparently!

As with all such high-profile appointments there were rumours about who was likely to get the job. Previous commission chairs had all been white men – David Lane, former government minister; Peter Newsam, Education Officer of the ILEA; and Michael Day, Head of the National Probation Service. Would they appoint a Black or Asian man? Or a woman?

That was all part of the intriguing speculation in the autumn of 1992, with many pundits speculating about who would or should be appointed. One interesting article was written by broadcaster and journalist, Trevor Phillips, for the *Weekly Journal* under the headline: 'Who will take over the CRE?' and stated: "I have of course no inside knowledge of the list of candidates, but it doesn't take too long to work out who would be considered. There are several distinguished public servants who could do the job, but may be ruled out for different reasons. Dame Jocelyn Barrow is a crucial figure in broadcasting to be released from her post at the broadcasting Standards Commission and has proved herself a brilliant manager and public servant, but it is hard to see why the EOC would hand her over to the CRE willingly. Mr Herman Ouseley, Chief Executive of Lambeth Council is the most effective manipulator of bureaucracy, Black or white that I have ever seen. But his association with Lambeth Council and the GLC may make it a political problem for Mr Clarke (Home Secretary). That would be a shame. He should be allowed to compete on the same terms as everyone else. Miss Usha Prashar, who has run the National Council for Voluntary Organisations and before that the Runnymede Trust, is said to be interested. She would be a formidable candidate. Mr Linbert Spencer, the former boss of Project Fullemploy, the training organisation, would also be a front runner. Mr Spencer has the most hands-on experience of race relations, and though charming, can handle himself in bureaucratic and political battle"

One actual high profile candidate not on Mr Phillips radar was none other than Jeremy Thorpe, the former leader of the Liberal Party, who I assume fell at the first hurdle.

The recruitment process was long-winded. I got through the first interview, but the next stage was held up because, it was rumoured, the home secretary was not keen on seeing the final list of appointable candidates, having already decided who he wanted in the job. My interview with him lasted twenty minutes. It was enjoyable, but I felt as if I was simply going through the motions, especially when his secretary entered the room to remind him that he was running late for his next meeting with the chief secretary of the Treasury. I was, therefore, relieved when the process was over. I had given it my best shot and it was another new experience I could build on. Having set myself up for the inevitable rejection and come to terms with being overlooked, I was astonished when I was told that the post was being offered to me. Somewhat in shock, I thought, "Do I really want this job?" I sounded out trusted colleagues and activists, who were equally surprised and urged me to think carefully before taking it on. Despite everything, I decided to accept the position, but only if I was assured that I could do it on my terms for the benefit of race relations in Great Britain.

Having accepted the new position, I became a lame duck at Lambeth Council but there was still five months to go to complete my contract. The political atmosphere there was still frenetic and scary. Trust and confidence at the top tier of the organisation was almost non-existent. One of the directors, widely regarded as a maverick operator and keen to elevate himself into my soon to be vacant position, bombarded me each morning with cleverly written, long-winded memoranda. He had a penchant for creating conspiracies around local historic incidents, putting them into a narrative that created suspicions, rumours and speculation about alleged ongoing and unproven corrupt practices. He would never name anyone and I, in my own state of confusion, was convinced that his motive could have been to deflect attention away from his own perceived shortcomings. He was also creating conflict, confusion and diversion, while convincing the powerful decision-makers that only he was capable of running the council effectively. After I had gone he got his moment, in an acting capacity, but only for a limited period. After that, he became a Houdini-like individual, who seemed to disappear without trace.

The intrigue, plots, counter-plots and suspicion continued to the end, but still many services were well run on a day-to-day basis. Some of the new initiatives were applauded by residents and local organisations but, in the end, I failed to remove all the rotten apples in the barrel before my departure. It was a sad moment for me because I loved Lambeth and still do. It had been a huge part of my working life and I had met some superb people including John Trotter and Chris West, who were among my very best and cherished friends. It was also reassuring to see that the council's equality profile had improved with increased numbers of Black, Asian and other ethnic minority people, disabled people and women on committees and as staff, some even occupying senior positions. I was also fortunate to have had in my corner at crucial moments many excellent support staff with strong commitments to public service ethics, with equality and fairness as integral parts of their everyday activities.

At the CRE a new reality began, bringing with it different challenges and more media focus, detailed attention and exposure. Awaiting my arrival was a stack of hate mail, much of which wanted to see the Commission shut down. Different racial groups criticised each other, and all sorts of allegations were made in an attempt to undermine the organisation, its staff and its reputation.

At the very beginning of my tenure, a very interesting and timely co-incidence connected me and the CRE with Lambeth and was to cause some consternation. It involved a former employee of Lambeth Council who was summarily dismissed by the chief executive of the council in 1990, which was before my arrival. The employee, who was Asian, was a known serial complainant who became a serial litigant over the years.

The previous Lambeth chief executive had always acted on instructions from the leader of the council and, when told to get rid of this employee, did so. The sacked employee claimed that his dismissal was unfair and sought the assistance of the CRE to fight his case and contest the matter in the employment tribunal. The former employee had a number of employment tribunal cases pending, none of which directly involved me until the week before my departure to the CRE. The council had a major flaw in its defence and did not offer much rebuff to the allegations. It was a case of the director of legal services determining, in his wisdom, not to even attempt to defend the indefensible. He also held the view that it would cost more to defend than to accept the penalties likely to be applied.

Inevitably, at one hearing, the employee received a financial compensatory award and a recommendation of reinstatement to his original post. The problem facing me as I was about to take leave of Lambeth was that reorganisation of the council and the reduction of the workforce made it impracticable for me to implement the former employee's demand for reinstatement. I made it clear that the department where he had worked had been reorganised and, due to budget pressures, there was no basis for his reinstatement. He immediately lodged a new discrimination claim with the tribunal against the council naming me, as chief executive, as a respondent. He also asked the CRE to investigate his claim that its incoming chair had racially discriminated against him, both as chief_executive of Lambeth and also as the new chair of the CRE. The latter allegation was based on his assumption that I had persuaded the CRE not to provide him with the legal support he sought from them. The Commission had indeed turned him down prior to my arrival, but this was unknown to me.

So, what a welcome! The new CRE chair was being investigated for racial discrimination before he even started. I found myself being investigated thoroughly, and thankfully I was cleared. But it was not over. I asked the CRE's legal officer to explain why support had not been approved. He said that the complainant's case did not fall within the CRE criteria for assistance and, in any event, the Commission lacked resources. I made it clear that it was not acceptable to me that cases were turned down on the basis of a lack of resources, and priorities would have to change. In this particular case, and in spite of the CRE's decision not to support the applicant, I argued that, whether or not his case was 'strong enough', he must be supported. If we did not, the CRE could be perceived as complicit in an act of discrimination and, in any event, the previous decision to turn him down had nothing whatsoever to do with me and it was necessary to clear the matter up once and for all.

After that, I contacted Lambeth Council's new acting chief executive to see what scope there was to collaborate and bring this sad case to an end. Both organisations were incurring costs unnecessarily. She was unaware of how much the council was liable for, as the director of legal services had kept all such information to himself. She agreed to look into the matter.

Their legal director had advised her that this particular discrimination case had cost the council around £17,000. Astutely, she was aware of the difficult characters she had to deal with at corporate management level and put her trust in a relatively junior staff member, who stealthily investigated and discovered that the actual cost was closer to £90,000 over the years of attrition. She acted immediately and suspended the legal director in his absence, securing his office over the weekend.

Her suspicions of unprofessional conduct were soon to be confirmed as the documents discovered revealed incredibly shocking activities, worse than suspected or envisaged. There were invoices for private detectives and costs incurred for phone bugging of the chief executive's office, home and elsewhere. She had achieved what I failed to do and nailed one of my tormentors. I was not paranoid after all, and it was good for me, at last, to know what was going on and who else was involved in the conspiracies, cover-ups and corrupt practices while I occupied the CE's position at Lambeth Council. The suspended officer was paid off eventually after at least two years at home on full pay, and the headlines in the *London Evening Standard* in May 1997 read: 'Council pays off top executive who ordered probe: £2 million wasted on snooping and nobody takes rap.' It took some time to start to get rid of the corrupt element in Lambeth. I had failed to nail them during my time, but played a part in helping to bring about their ultimate downfall from my new position at the CRE.

During my final days at Lambeth I was able to spend some time attending CRE meetings and meeting people from different communities and agencies across the country in preparation for lift-off in April 1993. Before my start date I had attended four Commission meetings, with the helpful guidance of the outgoing chair, Michael Day, and deputies Joe Abrams and Raminder Singh, who were also stepping down from office. During that time decisions were made to retain rather than combine the two deputy roles, not to appoint a new chief executive, to deal immediately with the budget and overspending and to launch formal investigations into the Council for Legal Education, Mobile Doctors Limited and the Benefits Agency.

I had already met the Home Office minister responsible for race relations – Peter Lloyd MP, Muslim leaders, the then Metropolitan Police Commissioner, Sir Paul Condon and the chair of the Select Committee on Home Affairs Sir Ivan Lawrence. Sir Ivan did not mince his words in advising me to pursue a softly, softly approach to race equality conflicts and issues. In his view the government would consider that a good job was being done if I was not knocking on the doors of Downing Street or putting a spotlight on controversial issues. He cautioned against demanding more resources and advised me to 'do good' by stealth and avoid high profile activity. It was not music to his ears when I suggested that problems in inner city neighbourhoods were bubbling under the surface and, without serious leadership and actions to end high unemployment and police/ community conflicts, the underclass of workless young people will not rest idly, to put it gently.

My first day was not good. I had a touch of influenza and early signs of hay fever and I was feeling a little groggy. Always an early starter, I was in the building before anyone else. The local shop-keeper opposite the CRE office alerted security staff to tell them that, "A man was seen wandering around the reception just after 7 am," and they came to locate me. Dramatic events always seemed to be scene setters during my first days at the CRE.

On day two I received the first of a number of anonymous death threats in the post, followed by menacing remarks from the extremist organisation Combat 18 during week two.

On day three the horrific race-hate murder of Stephen Lawrence rocked everyone to the core and led to an historic and titanic struggle for justice for Stephen and his family, as well as a challenge to the establishment about institutional racism. From the very beginning the police were in denial and made racist and stereotypical assumptions about Stephen and his friend Duwayne Brooks, who escaped with his life from the murderous gang. There was incompetence, cover-up and under-cover police infiltration aimed at undermining and discrediting Stephen's parents, Doreen and Neville Lawrence. At the CRE, we tried to get the home secretary to go and see the family, but he refused. Eventually, the minister, Peter Lloyd, did so after interventions by local MP Peter Bottomley.

There was a massive response to this racist attack with many active anti-racist organisations and local people challenging the local police for their failure to take the matter of racist policing seriously and about their apparent incompetence in pursuing the perpetrators. The CRE was denied access to information, even after meeting with police at Eltham police station. It was easy to be fobbed off with the response that the matter was being fully investigated and they could not waste time in responding to ours and others requests for information.

There was overwhelming public support for the family of Stephen and their loss. Stephen's parents, Doreen and Neville Lawrence were suddenly thrust into the frontline of seeking justice for the murder of Stephen. Their dignity and determination to overcome the odds stacked against them won over many people, who would not have previously believed that such murders were occurring and that the police were seeing Black young men as unworthy of being treated fairly, safely, trustworthy and entitled to justice. The rest is history as from that time, Doreen has been fighting for justice for Stephen and continues to use all her talent and energy in pursuance of a just and fair society for all. Her struggle is our struggle and she has been universally acclaimed and admired for her tenacity and achievements. The CRE's role was to a large extent, on the side-lines, trying to prod the police for visible effective action, to engage the leading politicians who were reluctant to become involved and had to acknowledge that we had no power to take on the police. Our support was for the family and their campaign for justice for Stephen, which had strong support from all sections of society. Eventually, it would have to be the politicians at Westminster who would have to act decisively and this only happened when in 1997, Jack Straw became Home Secretary, and responded to the calls from the Lawrence family for action. He then set up the Macpherson inquiry into the murder, which reported in 1999 with the findings of collective failures and institutional racism.

During my first week at the CRE, I urgently set about addressing my three main priorities for the organisation. The first was to get the 'overspent' budget back into balance and ensure that discrimination cases received the appropriate level of support. The second was to improve the image, reputation and credibility of the organisation. The third was to stimulate and inspire staff and commissioners to pursue the goals of race equality and better race relations with new vigour, ideas, sensitivity and intelligence.

I was inundated with requests to visit and meet with minority ethnic groups and communities around the country who were experiencing racial harassment and violence, as well as discrimination in the job market, at the workplace and in the housing sector. In my first three months my visits included sessions in Scotland, Wales, Leeds, Manchester, Coventry, Liverpool, Birmingham, Northampton, Bristol, Wellingborough, Reading, Sutton, Brighton, all parts of London and Torquay.

I appeared separately before both the Employment Select Committee and the Home Affairs Select Committee of parliament, met with the secretary of state for health and a back-bench committee of Conservative MPs who were cautious and anxious about what the CRE might be doing. There was no doubt in my mind that they were suspicious about my role and how I might lead the CRE. They were anxious to know that I would not be seeking to encourage any extreme responses to difficult situations, and were keen to be assured that we would be non-party political. All my public service roles had required professionalism and impartiality, so I had no problem with giving that assurance. However, because I was not one of their own, like all the other appointments, they remained suspicious.

I met around thirty of the eighty local Race Equality Councils, discussed race and sentencing with the Howard League and attended several organisations' annual general meetings to talk about the work of the CRE. Other contacts included the Indian Workers Association, the West London Synagogue, the Overseas Doctors Association, the Prince's Youth Business Trust, Muslim cultural centres and representatives from the ethnic press, criminal justice organisations, employment agencies, education organisations and too many others to mention. During this period there were three Commission meetings and we were sad to lose stalwart commissioners such as Kamlesh Bahl, Dipak Ray and David Lambert, but were delighted to welcome Dwain Neil, Bob Purkiss, Michael Hastings and Hugh Harris.

Significant internal change was also underway, preparing the organisation to take forward its new priorities and programme of work. Commissioners agreed a new

Impact Statement and established priorities for work on complaint handling and a complainant support network. Discrimination and inequality in the areas of employment and housing, racial attacks and harassment, formal investigations, tackling institutional and structural discrimination and work with and for young people were prominent among the agreed priorities.

An important inaugural meeting with all staff took place in May 1993, where they were briefed on the new direction proposed by commissioners. This included a commitment and determination to tackle low morale among staff and to improve communications internally and externally. We would also work to enhance the reputation, credibility and integrity of the CRE by adopting an exemplary and professional approach to all activities. All staff would be required to contribute to and uphold the standards of conduct expected as a statutory public service organisation. Our key objectives were to build credibility with the public and the people we served, apply the Race Relations Act within the spirit and letter of the law, and justify our existence through efficiency and effectiveness.

The scene was set and the key to delivery was leadership to build confidence and mutual trust within the organisation, with government and policy makers, with the CBI and TUC, with community and minority ethnic groups and with individuals seeking our assistance. We also needed to build better relations with all sections of the media, including those in the print media who often advocated our abolition. Above all else, the finances had to be sorted out. I was faced with budget cuts coupled with overspending in areas such as investigations and complainant aid. The new mantra which was at the heart of our Impact Statement was to 'Get more for less' as there was no other option acceptable to get us out of the hole we were in. This would require maximum input from committed staff; those who were not fully committed to the task and new direction were encouraged to look for new challenges elsewhere.

We sought support from external sources, and one of the best deals done, which was a win-win outcome for all sides, was with the renowned advertising agency, Saatchi & Saatchi. The CRE's planned high-profile campaigning and awareness-raising projects would benefit hugely from the creative involvement of Saatchi & Saatchi, whilst the company would be seen as fronting a major multicultural awareness-raising campaign that reached out to people from all backgrounds. The agency would thus reap the benefits of enhancing the equality image in the early stages of its global reputation. Importantly, it would be cost-free to the

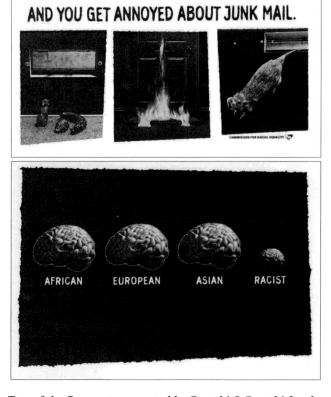

Two of the five posters created by Saatchi & Saatchi for the Commission for Racial Equality. Top: 'All Different, All Equal' was part of the European Youth Campaign Against Racism. Bottom: 'Uniting Britain for a Just Society', part of the CRE's campaign to raise awareness of racial discrimination and harassment in Britain.

CRE as contributions would come from Saatchi & Saatchi's flagship corporate clients which would also help in raising their consciousness about equality and race relations matters.

At that time the CBI, Business in the Community and the TUC had come together to tackle the issue of race equality within the corporate sector through the project, Race for Opportunity (RfO). Led by Robert Ayling from British Airways and involving Hugh Harris of the Bank of England, who was, a few years later, to become deputy chair of the CRE, the RfO was a very welcome initiative. We were supportive and offered help and assistance on good practice and compliance with statutory and voluntary codes of practice. However, we also made it clear that we would have no hesitation in taking enforcement action against RfO members, if warranted, on the grounds of either real or perceived racial discrimination at the workplace.

Partnership funding for joint projects and programmes was also explored, and the decision was made to bring legal services, previously contracted out, back in-house; the current arrangements were uneconomical given the strain the organisation was under as a result of annual government cuts. For me, these cuts were a case of déjà vu. Middlesex County Council, Greater London Council, ILEA – all had been financially squeezed and abolished! I had experienced Lambeth Council's austerity budgeting and now the CRE was being strangled to a slow death by annual budget reductions. But we had a plan, and it surprised the government each year as we survived and, indeed, did more with less.

This was not 'fake news' but still unbelievable in their eyes; we expanded when they expected contraction, opening offices in Wales and Scotland. We developed a range of other cost-saving initiatives. These included educational and monitoring tools to assist employers and service providers themselves to develop equality policies, implement equality programmes, train staff and monitor progress and achievements. We also produced documents on equality standards, with guidance for implementation and accounting for employment, housing, health and education. These were used by both private sector organisations and public service employers and users, local race equality councils, employees, trades unions and corporate managers. They helped to establish performance benchmarks for the development and implementation of equality programmes and monitoring arrangements without the need for day-to-day direct CRE involvement. In addition, we worked on initiatives with local anti-racist organisations and the police, all designed and applied to provide protection and advice for those who were being fire-bombed in their homes, having excrement put through their letter boxes, being abused and harassed on the streets and public places, in the workplace and on transport facilities.

One significant initiative, devised during the early months, survived the ultimate demise of the CRE and is still going today, operating as an independent charity but in receipt of financial support from the football authorities. When launched on 12 August 1993, it was known as the campaign, 'Let's Kick Racism Out of Football'. In those days racial harassment and abuse was rife, with many incidents going unreported. Hooliganism, racism and violence were features of football in England from grassroots and local amateur clubs right up to the top, elite levels of the game. Black professional players had to experience and cope with abuse and harassment, from their own team's supporters as well as opponents, often with no intervention made to prevent or stop this. Those who challenged or reacted against such behaviour often ended up being punished for their retaliatory and self-defensive actions. Black fans loved the sport, but the few who attended games would have to keep their heads down and put up with the racially-charged abuse that raged around them.

I know this from personal experience. I have endured such indignities and have felt humiliated when going into

Chairing the launch of the 'Let's Kick Racism Out of Football'
campaign in 1993. Pictured from left to right are former Chelsea
footballer Paul Elliot, Richard Faulkner of The Football Trust,
myself, Professional Footballers' Association (PFA) Chief
Executive Gordon Taylor and Wimbledon footballer John Fashanu.

football environments; being spat at or threatened with
violence, was common. For many Black, Asian and minority
ethnic people of my generation, we put up with this because
it was one of the few areas we saw Black people succeeding
– on the football pitch with skill, and defying the racists
with dignity, which we were proud to acknowledge and
admire.

The football authorities and most of the clubs appeared
oblivious to this disgraceful shame on their sport. When
challenged on the racism, the reaction was often that the
fans' conduct was based on ignorance, it was wider society's
problem and not football's and would change in time. Or
they simply denied it was happening. So, the Let's Kick
Racism Out of Football campaign was launched and evolved
into its current format as Kick It Out covering all forms of
discrimination. The CRE, the Professional Footballers
Association (PFA) and the Football Trust (now the Football
Foundation) joined together to get the ball rolling and the
campaign was established.

ELEVEN

Promises, promises, promises

By the fourth year of my five-year term as executive chair of the Commission for Racial Equality, I was contemplating the next phase of my working life, having been exhausted by the expansive targets, operational standards and goals set for the organisation. The CRE was relentless in its quest to be active in the community and build credibility and respect for its efforts to do more with diminishing resources as the government shredded its budget each year. Moderate progress was being made with public sector employers, less so with government departments and the private sector. Around fifty per cent of the eighty-two locally-based race equality councils were assessed as performing well. It was now 1997 and the Labour government, under Tony Blair, took the reins with Jack Straw as home secretary. Before coming to power they had promised to improve our grant aid but, when they set their first budget, we were to experience cuts – something they said would never happen on their watch. We strenuously argued our case but were told we had to settle for the same sum as the previous year, which still represented a cut because it did not take account of inflation. Following further representations on our part, the government finally agreed to provide an additional sum to cover inflation. That gesture offered hope of an end to the annual obsession with how to make ends meet when the demand for our services continued to increase.

Being effective meant having a presence in those parts of the country where there was the greatest need and local support for the CRE's work. Gaps were identified in Wales and Scotland and we opened administrative offices in Cardiff and Edinburgh. The work of local Racial Equality Councils (RECs) also made it easier to progress the CRE's work in those countries. Although our remit did not extend to Northern Ireland we sought to support committed activists and community representatives there who had campaigned tirelessly to have race relations legislation introduced, and resist those who argued that it was not necessary, "because there is no racism and few Black people here". In 1997, the Race Relations (Northern Ireland) Order had made it onto the statute books and work was underway to establish the Northern Ireland Commission for Racial Equality.

Nothing had prepared me for the intensity of the work to transform the fortunes and performance of the CRE. Previous chairs had their own styles of leadership, ways of managing staff and working with appointed Commissioners. They had to experience much public and community criticisms for the ways in which they had to respond and deal with conflict and confrontations and a rapidly changing demographic and legal framework. My own experiences mirrored theirs in some ways as the more you did was still never enough, and whichever direction you took to meet emergent challenges there were sceptics branding you as either uncaring or incompetent.

My personal and professional approaches have always been underpinned by a public service ethic ingrained in me through my career in working with and for people with public service needs. It was also necessary to absorb all reasonable criticisms and respond to them with rationality and appropriate actions. The people had high expectations, and I always found that responding with explanations and treating them with respect, except when you were being personally abused, enabled me to drive myself harder in support of our equality goals in trying to satisfy unrealistic expectations, such as eliminating racism from British society.

Most specifically, the central thrust of all our efforts was about rebuilding trust, confidence, credibility and integrity in an organisation created to tackle racial discrimination and to promote equality of opportunity and good race relations. There was a realism about understanding what was possible to do, what was possible to be achieved and what was not. We had limited power, limited resources and relied on persuading those with power and resources to do the right things. Having forward-looking race equality and race relations legislation enabled leading politicians to glow with pride, but they would avoid prioritising the essential actions required to implement policies, programmes and enforcement of legislation. That required not only moral but also responsible leadership, and very few leaders wanted to go the extra mile.

I appreciated the opportunity I had been given as chair of the CRE and there was not a second in the day that could be wasted, otherwise failure would be the inevitable outcome, something I rarely ever contemplated as a possibility. The number of meetings to attend, consultations to undertake, representations to make and events to appear at was endless. However, there was never a day in which there were not battles to be fought, some with the very people you are working for, those who are supposed to be your supporters and even your own staff and fellow commissioners. The most frustrating part of all was the relationship with government; speculation abounded about its lukewarm support for the CRE. Some observers speculated that the pre-1997 Conservative government believed the CRE would wither and die through incompetence and ineffectiveness, aided and abetted by annual reductions to its budget. Part of the analysis of that theory was the suggestion that I had been specifically appointed to destroy the CRE. There was an expectation that I would be reckless and careless in handling controversial issues, which would lead to the CRE being brought into disrepute and lead to calls for its abolition.

This was certainly something that concentrated my mind at all times. I could not afford to be reckless in actions to meet community requests to be more radical and put the CRE's existence in jeopardy. Heaven knows that I was cautious and professional at Middlesex County Council, the GLC and The ILEA and all three were abolished by governments. I hasten to add, abolition was not because of me, but the CRE's demise would not be under my watch. Nevertheless, my actions had to be bold and fearless, with my own brand of responsible leadership, to overcome all the critics accusing us of being toothless and irrelevant in the struggle for racial equality and justice.

Negative news coverage was also a constant threat as some journalists and politicians used every possible opportunity to be critical. There was always some adverse coverage almost every time we won battles in discrimination cases. We were not to be put off by such endless criticism as we pursued our legal obligations to raise awareness about racial discrimination, especially in the workplace, and encouraged increasing numbers of people to complain and to be supported in winning cases of victimisation and discrimination. The more we did, the more retaliation came our way. The terms 'political correctness' and 'compensation culture' became popular every-day jargon and were used to discredit both the CRE's work and the individual complainants whose cases had been won.

Our public awareness and advertising campaigns were being effective as they were deliberately and rightly controversial to get people's attention. The public would be alerted to issues around the existence of racial prejudice that resulted in individual and institutional racial discrimination, and prompt them to accept that they could and should do something about it. It was all about raising awareness and triggering a sense of personal responsibility to do something positive whilst avoiding using personal prejudice to discriminate unfairly and unlawfully. The posters on hoardings, on the London Underground and in full page advertisements in newspapers, aroused some hostile responses. But, nevertheless, the campaign succeeded in generating discussion and raising the profile about the existence of prejudice and discrimination. Racism would never be eliminated unless people recognised the problem and were persuaded that they had a part to play in tackling it. This would have to happen alongside actions to confront institutional discrimination. That was the core strategy applied in facing up to the reality of a changing world and a changing demography, towards changing public and political attitudes.

The politics impacting on race equality was polarised. Strong views, one way or the other, emerged from mainstream political parties and there were extreme racist and fascist organisations who wanted to end immigration, repatriate those who they determined did not belong here and shortlist different Black and minority ethnic groups for expulsion. There were anti-racist organisations that wanted the CRE to be more strident and overt in challenging the politics of denial, take formal action against institutions of the state and mobilise street activities to drive the racists off the streets. Then there were those who claimed that the CRE was only interested in inequalities and discrimination experienced by Black and Asian people. When we showed them that we handled cases of discrimination and provided support to white people of English, Scottish, Welsh and Irish national origins, the critics would retort that the this was only happening because we had run out of Black and Asian people and now needed white claimants to justify our continued existence. In reality, the CRE responded and reached out to all groups of people across Britain to ensure equal access and opportunity, regardless of their race, colour, ethnicity, nationality or national or ethnic origin. Whatever someone's race, we were there to help.

The opposition to the CRE and the constraints to maximum operational effectiveness did not diminish during my years as chair. There was political indifference and high-profile and influential criticism of our style and existence. There was substantial institutional inaction on the need to effect organisational change to end discrimination in public services and the corporate world, as well as in employment and the criminal justice system. The CRE did not back off, even when threatened, and maintained a relentless focus on building momentum among community organisations and inspiring local Race Equality Councils to do more and better with less resources. That was fundamental in my view as it was an uncompromising approach essential for survival. We had to build strong partnerships with prominent leaders in society and encourage them to take positive measures on equality and discrimination. We had an obligation to demonstrate the benefits arising from all equality based actions through personal, professional and responsible decision-making. To do this we established the Leadership Challenge which was launched by the new chancellor, Gordon Brown, soon after the Labour government was elected in May 1997. Many corporate leaders were persuaded to sign up on the basis that they would take personal and professional responsibility to drive change for equality and non-discrimination in their organisations, but they were the committed few and not the many needed to meet the challenges. Undoubtedly many would have signed up to support the leadership campaign as that was an easy win for their organisation's image, but were not necessarily wedded to the notions of eradicating racism. But it was a start.

Undoubtedly, there was a mood of optimism about race equality work following Tony Blair's landslide victory. That was unsurprising as people were desperate for new leadership. However, some of the anticipated expectations often bordered on the ridiculous as there was no way that the elimination of prejudice and discrimination was imminent. In spite of all good intentions, in the short term they were never going to change the embedded and historic culture of resistance toward ending racism in any

With the Speaker of the House of Commons, Betty Boothroyd MP
(now Baroness Boothroyd), hosting a function in support of the
CRE's 'Uniting Britain for a Just Society' campaign and the
'Leadership Challenge' project at the Houses of Parliament in 1997.

sustainable way, and so it was to prove. There was excessive
power in the hands of many unaccountable decision-makers,
and leading politicians would often back away, particularly
if, deep down in their hearts, ending racism was not
something they were prepared to go the extra mile for.

I admired and respected the often maligned former
premier, John Major, who conducted himself with integrity
and honesty in dealing with these matters. He expressed
what I believed to be genuine care about people who were
suffering unequal treatment. However, he was then deeply
ensconced in leadership struggles and disputes with his
anti-Europe colleagues that would ultimately contribute to

his exit from 10 Downing Street. I don't think he was ever going to rock the boat in favour of serious challenges to end institutional racism, but he was always supportive of us and condemned all forms of discrimination and racism. Nevertheless, we still suffered budget cuts each year during his time in office, and his personal support of CRE did not generate any positive actions from his government to tackle the deep seated problems that were sustaining institutional discrimination and unequal treatment of racial and ethnic groups of people.

The 1997 general election had seen the Labour Party sweep to power. The 'Four Tops' of the 'New Labour' hierarchy – Tony Blair, Gordon Brown, Peter Mandelson and Alastair Campbell – were quick to be seen embracing all the virtues of equality; but they all had bigger goals and their own cherished priorities to pursue. The challenge of tackling race inequality was, therefore, passed to the new Home Secretary, Jack Straw. He was quick to react, responding with a show of authority and commitment by ordering a public inquiry into the racist murder of the teenager, Stephen Lawrence. The inquiry was led by the retired High Court judge, Sir William Macpherson and he was advised by Tom Cook, a retired deputy chief constable, Dr John Sentamu, the Bishop for Stepney, and Dr Richard Stone, the chair of the Jewish Council for Racial Equality. The inquiry was welcomed by trade unions, community activists, politicians from different parties and even the British media.

The Stephen Lawrence Inquiry Report was published in 1999 and led to the Race Relations (Amendment) Act of 2000. The report concluded that the investigation into the killing of Stephen Lawrence had been "marred by a combination of professional incompetence, institutional racism and a failure of leadership". Specific officers in the Metropolitan Police were named and the entire force was criticised. The now famous definition of institutional discrimination reads: "The collective failure of an organisation to provide an appropriate and professional service to people because of their colour, culture or ethnic origin. It can be seen or detected in processes, attitudes and behaviour which amount to discrimination through unwitting prejudice, ignorance, thoughtless and racial stereotyping."

There was a knee-jerk reaction from some in the police service who objected to the perception that all Met police officers were racist. On the other hand, many police leaders did acknowledge that evidence pointed to a service in need of a total cultural change that would improve performance in policing, in order to help solve crimes but also ensure that all sections of the population were treated fairly and equally. Confidence in the police was low in Black and Asian communities, who were reluctant to co-operate or even report crimes, but without the trust and confidence of all communities the police could not claim to have the public support it needed to become an effective service.

Yet, in other sectors there were many positive initiatives. For instance, Eddie George, when governor of the Bank of England, convened meetings of recruiters in City of London firms who admitted mostly recruiting from sources that brought them candidates who were 'more of the same'. Why change, they asked, when they always got the people they wanted? However, the consequence of this was a workforce that was predominantly white and male with little or no access to opportunities for Black, Asian and other minority ethnic candidates. A few would have been motivated to change practices in their organisations, but the reality was that it required responsible leadership in all those firms to sign up for the Leadership Challenge and deliver the change themselves. Without that commitment and sustainable follow up only slow drip-by-drip progress would occur.

Another example was in the armed forces. Prince Charles and General Sir Charles Guthrie, head of all the services, were both determined and committed to seeing visible diversity in the armed services. I met with both of them at St James's Palace on 25 November 1996. Many tri-service meetings were convened to push forward changes to recruitment processes and the mono-cultural image of the services, which was off-putting to minority ethnic potential recruits. There was emerging evidence of the brutality experienced by Black and Asian recruits who were driven out of the services, and some of whose cases were the subject of tribunal disciplinary proceedings and some media coverage.

The situation in the armed services led to the CRE launching a Formal Investigation into the army, in particular, the Household Cavalry. A formal investigation was a legal process under the Race Relations Act 1976 that included a provision enabling the CRE to issue a Non-discrimination Notice which, if not complied with by the recipient organisation, could result in a court sanction. As an initial step the CRE could make inquiries and request information to enable it to demonstrate that it had sound reasons for commencing a formal investigation. During this time the employer or investigated organisation could take practical steps to adopt and pursue practices deemed to be fair and in accordance with recognised non-discriminatory good practices. At the end of its inquiries, if the CRE continued to hold the view that the organisation was in denial about discrimination, then it could institute the Formal Investigation process, set out the action required and ultimately, if appropriate, issue a Non-discrimination Notice. We regarded a Formal Investigation as a last resort since we could get more positive results by using it as a threat while working with organisations and their discrimination-deniers, providing advice and guidance and getting them to confront their prejudices and embrace the positive benefits and outcomes to be gained from change programmes for equality and inclusion.

The Household Cavalry of the royal household is part of the crème de la crème of the military. Prince Charles had been reported as saying that each year at the Trooping the Colour on Horse Guards Parade he never saw a Black or Asian face on parade. He wanted the service to reflect the community. But when the CRE made its move to challenge the army, the Ministry of Defence wanted to 'declare war' on the CRE as it rejected the claims of widespread discrimination and defended the indefensible, even in the face of irrefutable evidence. While respective heads of service expressed a commitment to overseeing the necessary changes in policies, practices, culture, attitudes and behaviour, resistance persisted in some areas and the pace of change was pedestrian. The impetus for action came with the change in government and the appointment of the new Secretary of State for Defence, George Robertson, and his ministerial team.

We embarked on the initial stages of the investigation, which was headed up at the CRE by Commissioner Bob Purkiss backed by Dwain Neil, also a commissioner, and supported by CRE lawyer, Barbara Cohen. During the lengthy Formal Investigation processes, there was an expressed commitment from the Household Cavalry Chiefs to undertake progressive work to ensure that the organisation moved toward becoming a non-discriminatory body.

One initiative involved outreach work to build relationships with Black, Asian and minority ethnic communities to make them aware that the armed services wanted them to sign up and be part of the British military. The project aim was to be all-embracing across minority ethnic communities so that they could envisage diversity as an integral part of the armed services. This day to day work was done mainly by a young Asian male secondee from the army, originally from the West Country but based at Horse Guards during his secondment. Progress was being made with visits to all parts of the country, to mosques, temples, youth clubs, community organisations and schools to generate interest and encourage applications. Just as his secondment period was coming to an end he raised with me his concerns about being sent back to base by the new major general of the Household Cavalry. This, he felt strongly, would have an adverse impact on the development and success of the outreach initiative, as it would be discontinued.

I immediately wrote to the major general drawing his attention to the achievements to date of the programme and asking him to extend the secondment in order to maximise these potential and actual beneficial and positive outcomes. He wrote back informing me that, "Rules are rules and the secondee must go back to base." I was incensed at such a ludicrous response. With utter impetuosity, anger and abandonment of etiquette, I scribbled with shaking hands: "That is bollocks! Rules may be rules but you can change them if you want to." It was sent to the major general instantly and without any further consideration or reflection on his likely reaction or the consequences. There was no doubt in my mind that he would not have responded in the same way to my original request if he was being asked to do so by someone like himself. I felt it was disrespectful and certainly stupid.

As my rage cleared and calmness prevailed I realised that my reaction would prompt a response that could probably lead to my dismissal. Expecting to be summoned to some sort of disciplinary hearing, I was shocked and relieved when I had the major general on the line the next day. "I have never received nor expected to receive such a bluntly abusive letter from anyone in authority. But, you're right. I can change the rules, but this equality stuff is new to me," he said. This was music to my ears, and to his too when I said to him, "If you are serious in wanting to make a difference, we are here to work with you and advise and support you with this initiative." He accepted my invitation to come to the CRE office in Victoria and I teamed him up with Bob Purkiss. They hit it off almost instantly, became very good friends and we responded positively to the major general's plea for help because, when challenged, he had not been slow in admitting that he needed assistance to do something that, up to that moment, was alien to him.

By the middle of March 1996, the CRE had found that the Army and the MoD had committed acts of racial discrimination following our Formal Investigation under the Race Relations Act into the Army's Household Division. Had the Armed Forces and Ministry of Defence accepted years ago the criticisms made of them by the CRE, the formal proceedings would not have been necessary. In welcoming the CRE's decision in 1998 to work collaboratively, the Minister for the Armed Services, Dr John Reid, said that they strongly believed that their continued good work in implementing robust equal opportunity policies was beginning to pay off as they were seeing an increase in the number of ethnic minority enquirers across the Services. On 25 March that year the CRE and the Armed Forces announced a five year partnership that committed both sides to working to promote racial equality practices across the Services. This agreement was unique and the first of its kind. It ensured an involvement of the CRE in monitoring actions and implementation of policies and programmes designed to achieve equality outcomes. Inevitably, when that five year period ended, it would be for the Services and its leaders to push forward with their equality activities, but progress would depend on responsible leadership, changing personnel, on-going political support and independent monitoring. In 2021, those components for responsible leadership are not always evident, and complaints from individual service personnel suggest that there is so much still to be done in the armed services to eliminate racial discrimination.

During 1996, the CRE had an exceptionally intense time when we started some exciting initiatives. We were devising, testing, experimenting and finalising proposals to deliver in the coming years. My five-year term as chair would end in 1998 and, therefore, I wanted the next two years to be action-packed so that, on my departure, we could hopefully demonstrate that we had delivered a range of sustainable achievements that would benefit future race relations in Britain.

An example of just one month in 1996 (July) illustrates the breadth and depth of activities and engagements we undertook. There were meetings with: the Council of Jews and Christians; the Inter-City Inter-faith Network; Runnymede Trust; Metropolitan Police; Better English Company; BME editors; English Heritage; Liverpool City Council; the Board of Jewish Deputies; Manningham Youth Forum; Youth Chamber for Sport; Windsor Fellowship; Irish Groups; the Littlewoods Organisation; the League of Jewish Women; the BBC on portrayal and representation issues; the Prince's Youth Business Trust; Childline, on children and racist bullying; the Welsh Language Board; Lewisham and East Staffordshire REC; and the Overseas Doctors' Association. Then there were events such as: Leicester City Football Club's conference for young people on racial harassment; a race and the media seminar and one on race and regeneration held in Manchester; a race equality event at the Bank of England with Governor Eddie George; Bristol REC's Respect celebration; and with Nelson Mandela when he became a Freeman at the City of London Guildhall, his visit to Brixton for Race for Opportunity and the Two Nations concert for him at the Albert Hall. We were at the launches of the Irish Report at the University of North London, a Multi-Agency Forum on Racial Harassment in Wales and our own *Roots of the Future* publication launched by Prince Charles and Anita Bhalla. We engaged with an Irish video project and a Kick It Out and Ark Theatre production and were part of the DFE Employment Advisory Group led by Cheryl Gillan, MP. Last but certainly not least we were in Bradford with Mohammed Ali and his QED organisation, involved in training, enterprise development and employment. We also managed to hold a Commission meeting out of London, in Manchester.

Meeting with South Africa's President Nelson Mandela at Brixton
Recreation Centre in south London on 12 July 1996. I am pictured,
from left to right, with writer and broadcaster Trevor Phillips, then
chair of British Airways and the Business in the Community's Race
for Opportunity project, Bob Ayling, Nelson Mandela, Prince
Charles and chief executive of Lambeth Council, Heather Rabbatts.

Not strictly a typical month's activities but fairly close
to everyday reality. 'Meeting and mixing' was my mantra
in pursuit of building better race and community relations
between people of all backgrounds. It was all about keeping
up appearances, maintaining momentum and enthusiasm
among local activists and decision-makers and agencies,
challenging racism and tackling prejudice and
discrimination. We recognised the importance of working
with others to improve race relations through increased
awareness, better education and knowledge about each
other and breaking down the walls of hostility by meeting
and mixing.

As the new Labour government entered office, we were
particularly interested to see how the new Blair, Brown and
Straw government would look – would ministerial
appointments be reflective of gender, race and ethnicity,
disability and sexual orientation? However, only Paul
Boateng from among the contingent of talented Black and

Asian MPs was awarded a position – that of minister for health. The ethnic minority media showed great interest in issues such as political representation, and at a London-based media event on 13th July at the Royal Festival Hall in the South Bank Centre, I was engulfed in a private heated discussion about race, politics and the media. I was repeatedly asked for my views about the new government and its approaches to ending racism. Eventually I offered a basic, "There appears to be tokenism and little or no Black in New Labour, but I shall reserve judgement until the autumn when a better appraisal can be made." I was clear that this off-the-cuff comment was made on a strictly confidential basis and I would only be prepared to go on the record after October when I would have had the benefit of six months to be better informed and to express a view. Little did I know that a journalist from *The Guardian* had been listening and my comment was to become a front page sensation the following week.

I was returning from an overnight visit to Leeds. My usual routine was always to get the first available morning train back to London in order to fulfil the day's commitments. I would travel so early that I usually did not have access to the day's newspapers. Just before the train arrived at Kings Cross station, I received a call from a colleague at the CRE who asked if I had seen the front page of *The Guardian*. The headline read 'CRE Chief Ouseley: No Black in New Labour!' Oh my God! I think I am again in big trouble! I was being asked to make a public statement. News print, radio and television were all desperately keen to speak to me but the feeling was not mutual. Worse, the prime minister was away on holiday and his deputy, John Prescott, was not around, so it was left to Peter Mandelson to let it be known that he was incandescent with rage and wanted an urgent explanation from me. One was offered informally, but we could not meet face to face until 4th August, so that was a tortuous waiting period full of anxiety and anticipation. In between, I was grateful to receive many messages of support and, when the dreaded day arrived, I was hoping that the heat and rage would have subsided with the passage of time. The initial greeting was cordial, and then he went full blast for the jugular. I tried to stay calm when providing my explanation and beliefs. I felt that he wanted me to feel as though I was appropriately admonished before moving on to be generous in sharing his views. Essentially, his plea was that I give the party more time before passing judgement. It was a sort of conciliatory outcome all round. Of course, that is what I thought I was doing until I saw that sensationalist newspaper headline!

It was not to be the only confrontation I had with the government. There were clashes over resources with the Minister for Race, Mike O'Brien MP, although he was always supportive of our work and, rightly, questioned matters where he had concerns about our approach or the outcomes from programmes and projects. A particular problem for the home secretary was the fact that my term of office was due to end, in early 1998. I was asked to consider a second term but was reluctant to accept. Under some pressure, I agreed to stay on for a reduced second term of two years to end in early 2000. I was duly awarded an unwanted full second term, scheduled to end in 2003. However, I was adamant that I could not possibly continue beyond 2000 because, by then, my energy levels would require massive re-boosting.

With head held high I walked away from the CRE in 2000 as I had planned. I was reasonably satisfied with my efforts, contributions and achievements, but sad to leave good people behind, and regretful that I had not changed the world or solved many of the race equality conundrums. I was, however, happy that I did not preside over the abolition of yet another organisation, and that I had not shrunk from the challenge out of utter personal frustration and the race prejudice and hatred still in existence. The CRE was in a better position than when I arrived. The Deputy Chair, Hugh Harris, took over the reins temporarily until the appointment of Gurbux Singh, who was previously the chief executive of Haringey Borough Council. He departed the CRE within a year to be followed by Trevor Phillips, distinguished broadcaster, chair of the Runnymede Trust, chair of the London Assembly and a former Labour Party candidate for the inaugural elected mayor of London in 2000.

TWELVE

Race off the agenda

W hen I left the CRE in 2000 it was to embark on a business initiative and set up a small advisory consultancy, the Different Realities Partnership, with a former colleague, Bob Purkiss, who was my main business partner. We were also fortunate to call upon Sheila Rogers, with whom we had both previously worked. She was particularly valuable when we had major assignments to undertake. Sheila offered invaluable insights and experiences from her own impressive leadership of the Northern Ireland Commission for Racial Equality, subsequently with the CRE in GB and during the formation of the Equality and Human Rights Commission. She also had an exceptional range of contacts and connections across the entirety of the equality and diversity policy and practice spectrum.

Bob's negotiation and relationship skills, gained from years of working within diverse workplaces and as a trade union organiser and senior officer, blended perfectly with our objectives and goals. My intention was always to run the business for five years and then move on. Both Bob and Sheila also had their own consultancies which outlasted my initiative. The ultimate aim was to generate interest and positive responses to the new impetus to bring about change in organisations with the principal goal of achieving equality, inclusion and cohesion in the workplaces and in the delivery of public services. One initial potential client was a leading investment bank. It boasted about being the biggest, the best, the richest and the most successful. Through a personal contact I was invited to talk to them about 'doing diversity' but when I asked what they understood and meant by this, no satisfactory answer was forthcoming other than, "Everyone was doing diversity so why not them?" I knew that this wasn't for me when they said, "Money is no object." This was the 'accepted' way that individuals were brought into organisations to give the impression of their commitment to "equal opportunities" Although I talked to their management group I could not be bothered even to claim out-of-pocket expenses as it appeared to me as just an exercise in 'fake diversity'.

During this five-year adventure I was even busier than I had been at the CRE. I combined voluntary and charitable activities with paid work and also acquired new duties having been ennobled in June 2001 as a crossbench life peer in the House of Lords.

I did not regard going to the House of Lords as anything other than an extension of my personal commitment to continued public service. Of course it was an honour to be asked and I welcomed the opportunity of experiencing life in the day to day work of the British parliament. I had no expectations of being in a position to change anything, although I did have my own views about the limitations of being part of an unelected chamber and was willing to vote for reform if it was to be a part of the political agenda. Of course, my Kick It Out voluntary chairperson activities continued and, even though I had expected to relinquish the role of chair some years before, I was so well ensconced in its routine that any likelihood of resignation was greeted with howls of rejection from committed volunteers and supporters. That was good for the ego but not good for family life, domestic responsibilities and involvement in family care responsibilities which seemed to be increasing daily.

The range of organisations I dealt with over the sixty months of Different Realities was extensive, and my work with them almost always involved management, leadership, discrimination, equality, inclusion and cohesion. There were investigations, reviews, reports and recommendations and giving talks, running seminars and participating on panels. Being a part of organisational inquiries or community based investigations were integral to my day to day activities and I had to reject more requests than I was able to accept.

Having left the CRE I thought I was taking back control of my life, but I became a sucker for a cause and it was virtually impossible to reject an opportunity to go into a new environment, identify its defects with regard to discrimination and exclusion and point the way forward towards effective equality outcomes. I produced on average two or three substantive reports in each of the five years, identifying and setting out the organisational responses required, but rarely was I ever involved in implementation or follow-up. My biggest regret was that, in nearly all cases, the organisations, their leaders, managers and decision-makers failed to implement key recommended actions. They would start a process of change and some would then desert it or obfuscate, rarely ever undertaking effective follow-up in measuring or managing progress. Even if the moment arrived when some measurable progress could be observed, complacency often kicked in as organisations believed they had cracked the problem and there was no need to worry any longer. On a number of occasions I received information from staff, and some managers, about the failure of their organisations' leadership to effect action in the way I had prescribed. Not surprisingly, such approaches failed to bring about change, or to embed an equality culture in the organisation, or achieve sustainable equality results.

One review I led, commissioned by the minister of finance and personnel on behalf of the Northern Ireland Executive, was into their procedures for selection and appointment to the Senior Civil Service (SCS). The intention was to identify the key issues and assess the effectiveness of procedures to make the compositional balance of the SCS more representative of the community. At that time, it was clearly evident that the SCS did not reflect the image of the diverse community being served, and was not likely to do so in the near future. The Northern Ireland Civil Service (NICS) had, on the whole, made measurable progress in representation in terms of gender and community background. It was not unexpected to identify instantly that the proportion of women and Catholics was higher in the lower grades and lower in the more senior grades.

The review undertook extensive consultations, examined the available data and pointed to a range of issues that required attention if obstacles to progression were to be removed. The Northern Ireland situation has its own historic complexities but it was accepted that change was necessary to ensure that the demands of devolution were met so that the NICS could command the respect and trust of the whole community. Our recommendations made it clear that success could only be achieved if there was responsive, dynamic and committed leadership from senior staff and elected representatives. They would have to demonstrate personal and professional behaviours in implementing a proportionate change programme that would yield sustainable equality outcomes. This is the bottom line for achieving any organisational change, whether in a corporate, public service or community-based setting. Those people with the power to make the decisions must want equality, inclusion and cohesion to happen, must know why it is not happening, how to then make it happen and must lead the change. If they do not, then change will not happen – that is the reality. History will shine a light on what changes occurred, how they were executed and what difference was made in achieving the desired outcomes on equality, inclusion and cohesion. But, without responsible leadership and commitment to change, the beneficial outcomes will be minimal.

Similarly, I was persuaded by Bradford Metropolitan Borough Council to lead a team conducting a review of race relations and race inequalities in this multicultural West

Yorkshire district. The Bradford Vision was a partnership of Bradford Council, West Yorkshire Police, Bradford University, Bradford, Keighley and Shipley Colleges, Bradford Chamber of Commerce, Bradford Health Authorities, Bradford Breakthrough, Yorkshire Forward and representatives from the voluntary sector and faith communities.

The decline in the economic base of that area had had an adverse effect on community relations and community togetherness. The manufacturing sector had gone, unemployment was on the rise, and new initiatives required public and private sector investment to revitalise prospects for a growing young population from diverse ethnic backgrounds. There were significant and growing divisions among the population along race, ethnic, faith and social class lines. People had become suspicious and fearful of each other. They were afraid of addressing serious or difficult issues, or even talking to each other. They were worried about saying or doing the wrong thing which could lead to repercussions and the unintended consequences of being labelled as 'racist'. There was anxiety about pursuing equality, inclusion and cohesion because of public and media criticism. There was crime and the fear of confronting gang culture, the illegal drugs trade, racial intolerance, harassment, abuse and violence.

The challenge was to establish an identity in the area that would embrace everyone and challenge the 'them and us' mentality. The promotion of pride in the district and its people, whatever their race, ethnicity, faith or social circumstances, was paramount. The fundamental question the review had to address was why was this fragmentation occurring? Why had there been a decline in community cohesion and how could people be brought together to halt the drift towards segregated communities? We conducted extensive consultations, referenced relevant studies and research and presented our report, 'Community Pride, Not Prejudice: Making diversity work in Bradford', in 2001. It focused on how different communities were heading towards self-segregation and highlighted the importance of education to tackle ignorance and prejudice. It urged the need to promote the many community-led projects and initiatives aimed at outcomes that brought people together and enabled them to learn from and with each other.

We recommended that Bradford's public services, including the police and other local and regional agencies adopt an institutional framework to tackle racial discrimination, social exclusion and unfair treatment to help arrest and reverse the trend toward segregation. In doing so they would also be meeting their obligations under the new Race Relations (Amendment) Act 2000, enacted following the Macpherson report into the murder of Stephen Lawrence. The approach would promote social interaction and provide opportunities for different cultural groups to meet and mix. Above all, it would require demonstrable leadership and decision-making at institutional, organisational and community levels to carry forward the mission and values that would lead to greater cultural and social interaction across the different communities.

The report did not meet with approval from all sides of the political spectrum on the council. Some interpreted our comments as criticism of them, and suspicion and speculation were rife. There was a danger that a blame culture would emerge, which was not helped by delays in publishing the report which were leading to yet more suspicion and speculation. Tensions were building locally among communities as a result of increased organised extreme racist activity in the form of threats, abuse, provocation and violence. It all became somewhat of a car crash when, before publication, the report's conclusions were revealed by the print media and on radio and television. This led to all sorts of forebodings, the most significant of which came to pass with the outbreak of serious disturbances in the form of community conflicts and riotous behaviour. There was extensive damage to property, facilities and injury to people. Around the same time, similar race related disturbances occurred in Burnley and Oldham leading to official independent public inquiries being set up by the Home Secretary Jack Straw. As a consequence thereafter, there was a plethora of projects emerging with their self-styled offerings of solutions in pursuit of better cohesion in those multi-racial areas.

Another review I undertook was for the Metropolitan Police Service (Met). I was asked by Sir John Stevens, the Police Commissioner for the Greater London Metropolis at that time, to consider how the service could build trust and confidence internally and between the police and the communities it served. Trust and confidence were two of the key defining factors identified by Macpherson's inquiry into the murder of Stephen Lawrence.

Eighteen years before Macpherson's report was published, the Lord Scarman-led inquiry into the Brixton Riots of April 1981, cited racial disadvantage, and criticised both the police and the government. However, Scarman's inquiry rejected the charge of institutional racism in the police service. The Macpherson inquiry, on the other hand, had no doubt that it existed and was the result of a collective failure.

Race and policing had been toxic for many years and would always be problematic while racial prejudice and racism existed. In the post-war period, in particular between the 1970s and 2000, there had been attempts by the police to use ethnic and racial profiling in relation to certain crimes.

Young Black men were particularly targeted as suspects in street crime. And this was the basis upon which the police used their powers of stop and search and the 'sus' laws – where the police required only a 'suspicion' that a person might commit a crime in order to apprehend or arrest them. This resulted in endless allegations of abusive and sometimes brutal police behaviour, and many instances of wrongful arrest and detention.

Over the years there were also many deaths in custody, which were deemed as further tragic symptoms of the hostile environment in which the Black community had to live. The mistrust and lack of confidence in the police had been no lower.

Corrupt practices and cover-ups also affected minority ethnic police officers – how they were treated, disciplined, had their grievances overlooked, were denied promotion and were driven out of the service. The Met spent hundreds of thousands of pounds settling cases on a confidential basis and with non-disclosure clauses, avoiding adjudication by employment tribunals and thus denying or accepting any guilt or liability. When challenged about settling discrimination cases in this way, they always sought to justify their actions by arguing that it was the least costly option for the Met and avoided lengthy, adverse publicity during Tribunal hearings. However, by not accepting liability for the actions of its officers, the Met had no reason to take disciplinary action against any staff, thus allowing them to continue working unchecked and without any investigation or sanctions.

Organisations which rush to defend themselves and deny allegations of discrimination, and reject action to avoid repeated allegations of misconduct, are deemed to be infected with institutional discrimination. The initial responses from some police forces to the Macpherson Inquiry Report indicated a service still in denial and, as a result, rejecting some of the recommendations. What was needed in the Met was purposeful and sustainable leadership, a clear intention to rid itself of corrupt and discriminatory working practices and a commitment to work with and for the communities it served to provide effective prevention and detection of criminal activity in the capital. This was what the incoming Commissioner, Sir John Stevens, set about doing and the Review, alongside other initiatives, was intended to assist him and his senior colleagues to begin to build trust and confidence within the service and with local communities.

It also needed to employ and deploy more Black, Asian and other minority ethnic groups. It had to be determined to tackle internal discrimination and to police by consent in consultation with the public. Therefore, the central thrust had to be visible, responsible and accountable leadership on equality and diversity from the top of the organisation, and reflected at different levels of the command and management structures. That was essential to achieve sustainable equality and inclusion outcomes which are integral for effective, fair and efficient policing. Our report was welcomed and its implementation carried forward through the internal management structures. How that was sustained after Sir John's departure is probably something for the subject of yet another review. Without sustained implementation activity led from the top, with monitoring and measuring progress and having open and accountable arrangements to enable independent scrutiny, there are clear opportunities to do nothing of significance. Yet there is a clear template to achieve the ultimate enduring benefits for the police service and the public it serves. If it does not happen it is clearly due to the absence of responsible and accountable leadership from the top and through the ranks.

I found a similar scenario when I was asked to review the increasing number of allegations and complaints from Black and Asian solicitors about what they considered was discriminatory treatment being meted out by the Solicitors Regulatory Authority (SRA), the body that regulates the conduct standards for the profession to safeguard the public interest. The main problem identified was disproportionality in the number of disciplinary proceedings taken against Black and Asian owned firms of solicitors. Other issues included the weight of compliance requirements imposed on small firms and sole practitioners, unaccountable inspections and investigations that led to suspension, the closure of businesses, the ruination of reputations, and the disproportionate costs associated with operating small firms compared to large city firms. There was also a dominant culture of secrecy of some SRA procedures without any reasonable access to proper scrutiny or accountability.

The review also considered and made recommendations to assist the SRA to improve its operational culture and processes and to build essential trust and confidence. It needed a more diverse and inclusive Board and workforce, and greater transparency and accountability, wherever practicable. As ever, responsible leadership at Board and Executive levels was essential to drive change if the SRA was to be seen as an effective and fair organisation with equality and inclusion at its core. However, to be successful such leadership has to be genuine, sustainable and responsive to opposition and obfuscation. It also needs to secure buy-in and ownership from all levels of management – failing to achieve this should never be an option. I was assisted by Bob and Sheila in this highly complex review and, after extensive analysis, consultations and hearing of the experiences of Black and Asian solicitors, we were able to put forward acceptable recommendations with implementable actions for their management to undertake.

In my view, the organisation should always own the implementation plan, develop their own action programme with expected outcomes and undertake the implementation themselves. What is more difficult and unacceptable for me is when I am asked to lead the implementation. Implementing action is an executive responsibility and not that of an independent external adviser. That, in my experience is an approach that allows executives to absolve themselves from their responsibilities. I was asked initially to do so by the SRA chief executive after completing the first stage review. I declined, informing him that he must own and lead all organisational change programmes. I often found that, when an outsider takes on this task, other staff tend not to view it as integral to the business, because the top brass are not seen as convincingly wedded to equality and diversity. They regard it as tokenism and a process that will be 'here today, gone tomorrow' – so why bother? If leaders pretend to be committed, start the process of change then leave it to others to carry the load while they move on to other priorities, then any short-term success or positive outcome will be temporary and too superficial to last. So the bottom line is, if you are a leader and you are not, yourself, making equalities happen with your own specific actions, then it will not happen!

In mid-2005 I closed down my business, as planned, to focus instead on my voluntary and charitable activities. By then it was clear to me that the 'New' Labour government had, to a large extent, abandoned the zeal for equality which had been evident when it came to power in 1997. It had moved into the newly discovered realm of 'light touch' regulation and deregulation, and this light touch was extended to the enforcement of equality law and practice. Macpherson's recommendations, the public sector equality duties, equality impact assessments and equality monitoring were no longer high priorities. Government departments are quick to sense the political mood and will back off without sustained pressure to change and be accountable, and so it was then. If regulation on equalities was no longer an imperative then there was no need for the executive to pursue the programmes with any enthusiasm.

It has often been cited that light touch regulation of the banking industry was a contributory factor to the financial crash in 2008. Nevertheless, in 2010, the incoming Coalition Government took de-regulation to new depths by effectively stripping away employees' rights to justice and putting this out of the reach of low-paid employees, most of whom could not even meet the newly introduced costs of lodging a discrimination claim at an Employment Tribunal. Aggrieved employees were required to negotiate several steps in seeking conciliation or arbitration of their dispute before even getting to the tribunal stage. The whole charade of the government's 'Red Tape Challenge', popular with employers and other deregulation supporters, saw the government renege on hard fought and deservedly won standards, regulations and procedures that protected the weakest and most vulnerable people. Such action and inaction directly contributed to the loss of focus on equality and inclusion programmes that would deliver beneficial outcomes for those who were discriminated against or treated unfairly in all employment related situations.

Austerity during the Coalition years of 2010-2015 and beyond hit the poorest communities hardest, in particular young people and families with young children. The demise of Sure-Start projects undermined opportunities for children to learn about themselves and those they mixed with in nursery education and care settings. Sure-Start had provided them with a grounding that prepared them for school life and gave parents the space to work and rest as well as fulfil their family responsibilities. Similarly, the closure of youth clubs, libraries and other social facilities left many young people, particularly those in deprived areas and those at risk, struggling to find the recreational and other meaningful outlets they needed in order to address and counter the disadvantage they faced. Nor were disabled people or the elderly prioritised and, indeed, often were exhorted to do more for themselves.

The carelessness and neglect of the government during the 2005-2010 period had been a pre-cursor for the subsequent depressing period of inequalities and reduced community cohesion and social mobility. During this time of de-regulation, the government presided over the demise of the Commission for Racial Equality, the Equal Opportunities Commission and the Disability Rights Commission and merged all equalities administration into the Equality and Human Rights Commission (EHRC). While there can be little doubt that this new body was created with the best intention of bringing about coherence across all the equality strands, warnings about the way the project was driven into existence were ignored and the ways of working, achievements and connections of the previous Commissions were marginalised. My main objection at the time was that setting up the EHRC was premature and should not have preceded the Equality Act of 2010. But, by the time this Act was in place, the EHRC was already established with its own distinctive new culture. Its structures and organisational culture had no room to accommodate the exceptional, locally-based equality initiatives, as its own priorities had a strategic focus with blue skies and wishful thinking. Had the Equality Act of 2010 preceded its creation, the legislation would, hopefully, have given credence to the establishment of a precisely defined regulatory and enforcement body to oversee the functions and duties of the Act.

Even before 2010, there was an increasing reluctance by the EHRC to challenge government departments on their failure to meet their equality objectives and targets in the post-Macpherson era which, if done effectively, should have led to a full onslaught on institutionalised discrimination. That this did not happen was due to the politics of complacency and arrogance in a government and leadership that had acquired a greater interest in global and foreign affairs. In my view, the EHRC's creation was little more than a government's a prestigious pet project that would enable it to boast about the UK's commitment to equality and human rights on the international stage.

After the Equality Act 2010 came into force, the Coalition Government had an open goal and could trample on all the good intentions and undermine the work of the EHRC. The EHRC had been promised an operational annual budget equivalent to the costs of the outgoing Commissions, but soon found that the government would slash its budget from an estimated £77m to £17m. Inevitably, the EHRC had to make difficult decisions. It discarded help for all but strategic cases of discrimination and focused on research, qualitative studies and Inquiries. While the Commission prioritised its work in meaningful and helpful ways, many people formed the view that it irrevocably disconnected itself from local communities and people's daily and real struggles for equality and everyday survival.

Whenever the government was challenged about its performance on equalities and deprivation and the adverse effects of cuts to public spending on poor communities, it was easy to deflect such criticism because there were few, if any, powerful champions campaigning on behalf of those people most affected by the government's policies. Prime Minister David Cameron's 'Big Society' initiative was one such policy, although it was short-lived as communities did not embrace his 'volunteerism' revolution. This was supposedly intended to remove power from politicians and put it in the hands of local people, although it was often criticised as masking a permanent reduction in state support for the needy. Cohesion was disintegrating in parts of the country and there were dire warnings from different sources about segregated communities and people living parallel lives. Much of this foreboding was rooted in the anxieties following the 9/11 attacks in the United States in 2001, the ensuing joint UK/US declaration of a 'war against terror' and the subsequent conflicts in Iraq, Afghanistan, Syria and parts of Africa, along with acts of terrorism on the streets of some major cities across Europe, including the UK.

An inevitable bi-product of this scenario was government developing a new domestic focus on equalities which, rightly, prioritised policies to deal with growing Islamophobia and hate-inspired attacks on Muslims. This, when put alongside debates about immigration (both EU and non-EU) and the campaigns of UKIP, contributed to the development of a toxic environment. The phenomenon of UKIP undoubtedly owed much to the charismatic leadership of Nigel Farage. Their stance on 'taking back our country', deciding who to let in, controlling the movement of people and making 'our own' decisions became a rallying call to leave the EU. It played to people's fears and prejudices and it was no surprise that support for UKIP grew mostly in those areas where families were under pressure due to poverty and austerity measures such as the 'bedroom tax', the freezing of child benefits and reductions in housing benefits. These would have been critical factors for people when they were considering how to vote in the EU Referendum of 2016.

Of course, immigration has never been off the agenda. Virtually every government since the Second World War has grappled unsuccessfully with trying to satisfy those who are obsessed with the numbers rather than the newcomers as people, where and how they settle and the contributions they make to the economy and wider society. In the years preceding the Referendum there was criticism of the Blair Government and its adherence to the principle of free movement but without any controls. The Coalition Government that followed made delusional promises to bring immigration under control and failed. The Cameron Government owed its election win largely to the promise of a referendum to leave or stay in the EU and the rest is history. At some stage in the not too distant future, people will reflect on this period of fundamental political and social upheaval and determine for themselves what role they played in the politics of Brexit and 'taking back control of our country'.

THIRTEEN

Football, bloody hell!

A lthough I had already moved on with the next phase of my life through my business consultancy, my new entrepreneurial ventures did not stop me from pursuing a range of voluntary activities. In particular, I continued as chair of the Policy and Research Institute for Ageing and Ethnicity, led by Naina Patel; Preset Education and Training Project, led by the irrepressible Captain Chandran; Kick It Out, the campaign to tackle racism and discrimination in football; a council member of the Institute for Race Relations; and patron of at least a dozen other organisations. I knew that I would run my business consultancy for no more than five years and, in fact, closed it in 2005. But I did not expect to be still chairing Kick It Out by then, and certainly not twenty-five years after I, and several other individual anti-racist supporters, founded the campaign, 'Let's Kick Racism Out of Football' in 1993.

I had taken the decision to mount the campaign, ultimately to be known as Kick It Out, in my capacity as chair of the CRE following discussions with some key staff and a few commissioner colleagues. There was clear justification for doing so. Black football players and fans were being harassed, abused and discriminated against without any apparent recourse to justice, and the CRE had a responsibility to tackle racial discrimination and promote good race relations. I had tried, unsuccessfully, on a few occasions to get professional clubs to take action. I had witnessed, as did thousands of other people, abusive incidents at games and heard first-hand from players about their treatment and their fears. There were some horrendous acts of violence, and I was deeply affected by the racial abuse of Black and Asian players and fans at all levels of the game. So much so, in fact, that I eventually decided to avoid professional matches altogether, despite my love of the game.

The professional players could not walk away, though. It was their livelihood and they wanted to stay in football, but were reluctant to go public with their grievances. They felt powerless in challenging their employers to effect their duty of care. I found the situation intolerable. I had tried on a few occasions to get professional clubs to take action, but whenever I complained to a club they would ask for the evidence – which I could not disclose, as the complainants, who spoke to me in confidence, would experience further detrimental treatment. So, I had to walk away with no accessible route to pursue further action. Those experiencing discriminatory treatment were not prepared to put their heads above the parapet, and those powerful and authoritative people running football remained unmoved and reluctant to act. With renewed determination, I searched for any possible opportunity to encourage the players to be bold, daring and assertive in openly challenging the game's complacent leadership and irresponsible hierarchy.

Then suddenly, my options changed with my appointment to chair of the CRE. I no longer had to walk away despondently, feeling that nothing could be done to tackle and change football culture. I now had a choice to do something purposeful or do nothing. Up until then I could do little, other than try to persuade the powers-that-be to take action against the racial abuse and violence, but I was now in a position of power. I now had the ability and legitimacy to challenge both the clubs and the football authorities.

At first, there was still little enthusiasm for taking action because clubs, leagues and leaders in the game were in denial about what was going on in and around all those in football. Indeed, I was accused by some of creating the problem. Having failed to enthuse many of those approached, I quickly moved on to the next step. I exhorted clubs to initiate action against their abusive supporters and drew their attention to the enforcement powers held by the CRE. This new approach coincided with the initiative to launch and run the Let's Kick Racism Out of Football campaign. All ninety-two professional clubs were invited to join. CRE colleagues initially led the approaches to the clubs, and it was determined that if we got fifty per cent positive responses, we would press ahead. We received the required number of responses within weeks but our ambition was to achieve 100 per cent participation before the end of the forthcoming season. We had to use smart tactics to get some of the big clubs to come on board. For instance, the then chair of Manchester United, Martin Edwards, said that they would be too busy to take part as they were now back in European competition, following the end of the UEFA ban on all English teams imposed after the Heysel Stadium disaster in Belgium in 1985 (an incident of fan violence that resulted in the deaths of 39 people). I therefore contacted Sir Howard Davies, the then chair of the Audit Commission, who knew the chair of Manchester City Football Club, and he persuaded them to join. After that, I was able to tell Manchester United that their neighbour would be part of the campaign, and to avoid the embarrassment of being perceived to be uncaring and unwilling to challenge racism, they too should sign up. Surprisingly, they had a change of heart and decided to do so. The fear of being named and shamed was a vital tactic that encouraged clubs to sign up for the campaign. Of course, there was a downside; they agreed to join a campaign but it did not mean that they would do much, if anything, to tackle the problems identified with any enthusiasm or purposefulness.

From the outset we targeted the Professional Footballers Association (PFA) to partner with the CRE in sharing the initial cost of the campaign, as the football authorities and clubs were reluctant to incur any cost. The PFA, led by Chief Executive, Gordon Taylor, was willing to be joint founders and funders and has stuck with the campaign since day one. We also secured a small but significant grant from the Football Trust (now the Football Foundation) and the launch went ahead. Initially, it was about t-shirts, badges, stickers, banners, newsletters, fanzines and leaflets. The campaign's sustainability owed much to adopting a gradualist approach. There was a desire to see effective actions and rapid change, but we had to be realistic in keeping clubs and enthusiastic campaigners involved. At that time there was no appetite for challenging what was perceived by football as a whole as some radical and unnecessary initiative.

Personally, my view was that footballers should have been outraged by what was going on and used their real power to initiate change by withdrawing their labour. (Hindsight now in 2021 shows that football is meaningless without footballers playing!). I remain convinced that direct action was as necessary then as it is now to achieve the equality and fairness required. However, common sense had to be applied in 1993 and we had to tread sensitively to avoid upsetting the good and the great (and the not so good or great), who really could have done without this mild campaign regarded by them as both unnecessary and irritating. After all, they held the view that there was no racial discrimination in football, everyone had an equal opportunity and all will be well in a matter of time without any external interference.

That was the context and climate in which we persevered and developed guidance on best equality and non-discrimination practices for supporters' groups to assist with their campaigns against racial abuse. We encouraged clubs to incorporate multicultural images in their advertisements and programmes and to employ Black, Asian and minority ethnic people as match-day staff, even though we knew this would be token numbers initially. We also looked to enlightened leaders in the game to introduce equality policies and programmes. It was piecemeal and fragmented during the early days, and I knew it could only take off and be a powerful force for race relations and change in football if some of the game's powerful big hitters started putting their heads above the parapet.

Luckily, some very prominent and influential friends definitely wanted change and came forward to add their weight to the campaign. They recognised the benefits to be derived for the game and would be active in trying to influence change in those areas where they were powerful. David Dein, who was then the vice-chairman of both Arsenal Football Club and the Football Association, as well as a someone credited with the creation of the newly formed Premier League and a global figure of enormous respect in the sport, offered support. Alongside him was David Davies, a director at the Football Association, who was prepared to speak up and give credence to the push for responsible leadership and action. But even though we had a newfound optimism, there were many obstacles to overcome. We had to stick with the gradualist approach if we were going to hang onto clubs' and the leagues' involvement. In reality, often their involvement was superficial, tokenistic and unworthy of the praise we accorded them for their minimalist efforts. Yes, much grovelling was needed in order to get things done. Unbelievably, in spite of the blatant abuse of Black players at virtually all the professional football clubs in England, some club directors and senior league officials continued to insist that there was not a problem, or at least the problem was being faced up to with their token minimal involvement.

As the campaign developed, action programmes and formal liaison arrangements with staff in some clubs resulted in joint work but, usually, it was relatively junior staff who were involved in these initiatives. They were associated with community related activities and uninfluential within the mainstream of the clubs' priorities. This approach was problematic and demonstrated a low priority among a club's commitments. It had the detrimental effect that, whenever a key member of staff from the community development side of the club left, no-one else would have a clue what race equality initiatives were being developed. Senior administrators, managers, coaches and board members were unlikely to know about the issues and were not interested – it was not important, not a high priority and so who cares?

We in the CRE and the PFA, and those community-based club supporters and anti-racist activists, were determined that Kick It Out should stand on its own, as an independent project. But we needed financial support in order to keep up some momentum, and we had to wait at least another year before the Premier League, the Football League and other leading lights in the game came on board. While I was at the CRE at least I had the legal enforcement weapon to use as a threat against the authorities and clubs, which were complacent and in denial. But I also had to safeguard the integrity of the CRE and not bring it into disrepute by any unreasonable approaches to the clubs for actions that they deemed to be unnecessary. I was cognisant at all times of my over-riding responsibilities as chair of the CRE, while also being the chair of the campaign at the same time, and conducted my dealings with the football authorities in a structured and professional way. However, once I had left the CRE, the shackles were off and there was no longer any reason to be gentle and ultra-sensitive with them.

By then, we were also beginning to connect with some of the more prominent players, many at the end of their professional careers, who were prepared to speak up and speak out about their awful experiences. These included people like Paul Elliott, who was previously captain of

Chelsea before a serious injury halted his illustrious career, Luther Blissett, Garth Crooks, Cyril Regis, Brendon Batson, John Fashanu, Ricky Hill, the Stein brothers and several others from that era. The government was also on the ball, introducing the Football Offences Act which made racial abuse and race hate violence in the game a criminal offence.

By the late 1990s, the CRE had, quite reasonably, concluded that it was time for Kick It Out to do its own thing without recourse to the Commission's limited resources. It was established as a specialist, charitable organisation that would enable, educate and initiate change in policies, attitudes and conduct across the game to tackle race hatred and other forms of discrimination. With a few staff and volunteers, advisory groups, independent trustees and representatives from the FA, the Premier League and the PFA (later to include the English Football League), Kick It Out was determined to get to grips with the lethargy in football that was allowing Black and other minority ethnic players and fans to be so disgracefully abused.

After I left the CRE in 2000, I was asked to stay on as chair of Kick It Out, and several unsuccessful attempts on my part to stand down from that position in subsequent years failed because it was always considered by others to be "a bad time to leave," or, "not now," and, "give it another year," and so on.

As an independent charity, Kick It Out's day-to-day leadership was the responsibility of the Director, Piara Powar, an experienced and seasoned networker and campaigner. A Race Equality Standard was designed, (later expanded to cover the other equality characteristics), to help guide clubs to adopt policies and practices and to manage and monitor their equality actions and outcomes. This framework provided them with guidance and best practice in the development and implementation of policies and programmes, and in charting progress for assessment and accreditation. It was introduced on a voluntary basis for all clubs, who could seek accreditation on the basis of verified evidence of their achievements. Most clubs kept their distance and were reluctant to embrace this new and progressive initiative until the Premier League encouraged all of its clubs to engage with the development stages of the Standard. Without this encouragement, it is likely that it would have floundered in the way that many well-meaning initiatives do when the full commitment of powerful and responsible leadership is missing. Some years later, the Premier League utilised its influence and commitment to persuade other football stakeholders to recognise the need for football to be in the vanguard of progressive change, utilising the power of the game in contributing to equality, inclusion and cohesion. This is nowadays the template for progressive accountable action administered by the Premier League and influencing the game, as a whole, to be on a par with the best performing corporate and public service organisations.

Responsible leadership encompasses progressive commitments and viable, decisive action. It is a key component in bringing about meaningful change, inspiring trust and confidence and generating the personal, professional and voluntary inputs that lead to equality outcomes. Kick It Out sought, at all times, to develop good working relationships with all parts of the game and at all levels including The Football Association, The Premier League, The English Football League, the Professional Footballers' Association and the League Managers' Association. It always kept the overwhelming hope that such 'responsible leadership' would take ownership of the equality, inclusion and cohesion agenda. That was the key to real change. Too many people, wrongly, would criticise Kick It Out for the failure to see progress, because they thought we had the responsibility and the power to force change where needed.

In reality, Kick It Out had neither the authority nor the power to make the internal changes that were required, and we were unable to persuade the decision-makers to lead the drive for equality and fair treatment, although this was not for the lack of trying. Players often criticised the campaign for failing to deliver what they considered to be required outcomes to address detrimental treatment, because they did not understand that we did not have the power to do so. The key to success was to get those at the top and in key positions to come to terms with their own ignorance and ineptitude, and understand and address their personal biases and the effects of continuing institutional discrimination and exclusion. This is not an accusation of personal or direct discrimination, but the reality of how each of us must address our own shortcomings if we are to make a positive contribution to ending inequality and discrimination.

Kick It Out reached out to the governing body of football in England for that leadership, the Football Association (FA), but it was not always forthcoming. During the twenty-six years of my involvement, each newly appointed FA Chair has offered commitment and pledged to bring about reform and become more inclusive. This would generate optimism that change might happen; however, they have all had to tread carefully and be extremely sensitive in their attempts to take forward equality proposals. The FA's historic, cumbersome structures, governance, shareholding arrangements and decision-making made it impossible for new incumbents to turn things around quickly but, to their credit, each chair has made some progress before passing the baton on to their successor.

I worked with different chairs, including David Treisman, David Bernstein and Greg Dyke and, it is fair to say, they were highly respected and credible leaders who always had the best of intentions. Each of them used their personal and professional qualities to nudge the FA towards becoming a modern, effective national governing body for football in England. The most recent, Greg Clarke, brought his own brand of enthusiastic and charismatic leadership and blunt-speaking, and offered hope of change when engaging with others to win their support. But in the end it was to be his bluntness, coupled with his own perceptions and interpretations of how to solve the problem of race and equality, which led to his demise.

Of course, the FA has had to endure some deeply embarrassing moments in recent times, not least the way in which the English international player Eniola Aluko was treated in a highly discriminatory way, the shambles of the dismissal of Mark Sampson (the former England women's team head coach) and the performance of the chief executive and chair in their encounter with the Parliamentary Select Committee for Culture, Media, Sport and Digital Services. In fairness to Greg Clarke, he did have a sincere understanding of the benefits that derive from the pursuit of equality policies and programmes. Before he unexpectedly imploded by making a series of discriminatory remarks about race and gender before the Parliamentary Committee, he helped to create a mood of optimism as the FA's equality, diversity and inclusion work moved forward with some programmes already yielding visible outcomes. Its main board is now more diverse and includes women and a splash of ethnic colour, and it is served by the Inclusion Advisory Board led by former England international player and former Chelsea captain, Paul Elliott. Clarke was also a champion to secure Paul Elliott onto the FA Board as a fully-fledged member, and deserves to be credited for his contributions in making the FA a better governing body on equalities than it was before he arrived.

Over the years, Kick It Out has had to tip-toe around to overcome the barriers that have prevented it from making the progress it should have been able to achieve. There have been many no-go areas, particularly when seeking evidence of inequality, discrimination and exclusion. Senior management, training grounds and coaching staff were out of bounds in virtually all clubs to Kick It Out, although there were some progressive administrations that were ahead of the rest in their equality and diversity achievements. Almost everyone in professional clubs had been most comfortable with equality and inclusion issues being administered at the lowly community level. They were more than happy for Kick It Out to work just with the community liaison personnel or their public relations or communications personnel. It is only in recent years that representatives from senior management have shown any direct interest in planning or implementing equality arrangements. Often, Kick It Out has had to rely on individual contacts and develop and use its own networks to penetrate clubs' internal management and administration, making headway by stealth and craftiness. However, it is clear that the presence of responsible and demonstrable leadership has been the key to Kick It Out's credibility, survival and success. This became most apparent when individual clubs began to understand and embrace the benefits to be derived from being an equality-accredited organisation that is inclusive and contributes to community cohesion.

In the absence of players feeling able or willing to take direct action to free themselves from the shackles of institutional racism within the world of professional football, those of us campaigning on the outer fringes had to tread carefully to make any progress. Winning hearts and minds and demonstrating the benefits of equality and inclusion were fundamental in making progress in the early days of Kick It Out's work, and this remained the preferred way of working to get clubs and their leaders to develop and implement their own sustainable initiatives. But it is nevertheless a slow and quiet option which has sometimes led critics to conclude that very little was happening and Kick It Out was ineffective. In the high-profile world of football, publicity was, and always will be, an important weapon in Kick It Out's armoury. Many excellent and well-motivated sports journalists have keenly covered racial abuse and other forms of hate-inspired incidents, thus making the public more aware of the extent and awfulness of the problem. This type of exposure was vital in keeping regulatory bodies and clubs on their toes, enabling Kick It Out to maintain pressure on the authorities and clubs to do more, and in the right way. Publicising our own activities and initiatives was another important ingredient in raising awareness among clubs, supporters and the wider public. It was always beneficial, although not always easy, to get top players to front campaigns whenever we could. We would always want to use the good and the great to front our equality projects as they were admired both by supporters and the next generation of players.

From the outset, we valued the educational and awareness roles of the campaign. We sought to utilise every opportunity to work with local schools, especially among the very young children. They were often the most engaging and most responsive. When we had the presence of leading football stars they all came alight with enthusiasm, and such events also generated positive publicity for the schools, the players, their clubs' supporters, local communities and the game as a whole.

An example of this during the 1990s was when Arsenal welcomed local school children to the stadium to hear about the life experiences of their superstars at that time, such as the French players, Thierry Henry and Patrick Vieira. They told of the abuse and discrimination they suffered, how much it hurt and how they dealt with it. The children were in awe of their heroes and were encouraged by their teachers to ask questions. Such days offered hope and optimism for the future as the young people learned to regard racial and other abuse as unacceptable, and supported strong interventions and sanctions to make the sport safer and discrimination-free. Their experiences sometimes fed into the overall school curriculum on citizenship, fairness and community cohesion, and how people should relate with each other, thus bringing about longer-term, positive benefits.

Excellent work has also been undertaken by the organisation, Show Racism the Red Card, which was launched in 1995. It takes its anti-racist programmes into schools and clubs, using current and past players as role models to talk about their experiences and to fly the flag for equality and fair treatment. Getting current players to attend these events has not always been easy for Kick It Out as there are so many gate-keepers – such as agents, managers, coaches and sponsors as well as the players' commitments to participate in events for their own clubs. In recent years, however, some have readily and enthusiastically taken on ambassadorial roles with Kick It Out, particularly during the earlier stages of their professional careers.

Perhaps Kick It Out's biggest coup in the early years was getting the legendary football club manager, Alex Ferguson (later knighted), to give the campaign a much needed boost. It was a wet night in south London on 7th March 1995 when Alex brought his high-flying Manchester United team to play Wimbledon FC at Selhurst Park (the home ground of Crystal Palace). The stadium was full of spectators in spite of the weather. Just before kick-off, a banner was unfurled in the centre of the pitch which read 'Let's Kick Racism Out of Football' and at the centre of those holding it was none other than Alex Ferguson, getting soaked in the downpour but evidently proud to be lending his support to the campaign. Joining him that night, in addition to myself, were Robbie Earl of Wimbledon, Richard Faulkner from the Football Trust and himself a Wimbledon fan, Gordon Taylor of the Professional Footballers Association and former Chelsea player Paul Elliott. Sir Alex Ferguson's presence and visible commitment to the struggles against racism and for equality and fair treatment in football sent out a powerful message of endorsement for the campaign. He had a formidable reputation for championing underdogs and challenging injustices, and was the first high-profile manager to step into the frontline of anti-racist struggles in football and to go where others feared to tread. During the rest of his highly successful career he was an exemplar in standing up for justice and equality in line with his values and principles. Other managers and coaches, especially during the early years of Kick It Out, were also prominent in giving Black footballers opportunities to succeed at the highest levels. These included Graham Taylor, David Pleat, Ron Atkinson, Peter Shreeves and Sir Bobby Robson. Many more have done so since, and it is now unusual to find any club or team without Black players as an integral part of their squads.

At board level, and especially at the elite club level of the game, there have been exceptional administrators, leaders and decision-makers who stood up against racism and racial abuse. David Dein, a respected figure globally in football, was strong in his support in the early days when he was with Arsenal and today remains a staunch supporter of Kick It Out. Bruce Buck, the chairman of Chelsea FC, worked tirelessly with the Russian owner Roman Abramovich, to shift the club's image from being associated with racial harassment, abuse and hate-related violence to that of an organisation now seen as an exemplar in tackling such evils, especially with regard to tackling antisemitism. Ivan Gazidis, when he was CEO at Arsenal, along with his manager Arsene Wenger, helped the club not only to have solid ethnic diversity on the field of play but also among supporters, both home and away. Similar plaudits can be extended to David Gill during his stint as CEO at Manchester United and the present administration at Liverpool FC in the post-Luis Suarez period.

There are others, but they all need to get their act together and learn from the exemplars.

In addition, the role of the influencers at the top cannot be overlooked. In this regard, mention has to be made of football's own modern iconic administrator, Richard Scudamore. He was a dynamic leader of the English Premier League for two decades. In his role of chief executive and executive chairman, he helped to make the Premier League the most envied professional football league with its riches and players from all over the world. In his own way, before his departure in 2018, he influenced his member clubs to embrace the values of equality. He exuded assuredness in what he said and did, knew what he wanted and why, maintained a focus on the outcomes to be achieved, got the job done and connected to the people he needed to be with him to get innovative proposals across the line.

It is the responsibility of those at the top of the clubs and the authorities, as the employers and the enforcers of rules and regulations, to act to bring about change, end unfairness in the system, tackle persistent discrimination and change the largely mono-ethnic profile so evident in virtually all their off-field operations. Kick It Out identified and drew attention to acts of discrimination and abuse, but had no authority over the implementation of the corrective and remedial actions that needed to be taken. When such action was not taken or sanctions were regarded as inadequate, Kick It Out would at times be blamed for these failures. It took many years of challenge and overcoming resistance to get complainants and victims of discrimination to understand the realities of the system and to turn their fire, frustration and anger on the authorities and the decision-makers who were failing in their responsibilities.

The organisation had to be resilient and manage conflicting situations sensitively and diplomatically but, at the same time, with strategic ruthlessness – not easy for a relatively small charitable body. The reality was that at any time you could be running positive education programmes at a club for players and other staff, while at the same time supporting complaining fans or employees with complaints or grievances whilst working with the club on positive inclusion programmes. Multi-tasking was a key requirement of Kick It Out's staff and volunteers. Kick It Out continually found itself supporting individuals who publicly criticised a club for recalcitrance in taking action against homophobia, anti-Semitism, sexism or other unacceptable behaviours, while at the same time advising and guiding the club on positive action initiatives. It is the sort of work that requires you to face in different directions simultaneously, but pursuing the same outcomes of fairness, equality and justice.

Partnership work was another fundamental part of the way Kick It Out sought to make progress with the football authorities and clubs, utilising the interests of agencies outside the game. Much of the campaign's deemed successes up to the time of my departure in 2019 owed much to the support of its principal partners the PFA, FA, PL and EFL, who were represented on Kick It Out's Board of Trustees and who have to implement the necessary actions for change and equality outcomes. Kick It Out also worked closely with the League Managers' Association, LMA, and has undertaken joint initiatives with many others in the game at professional club level and in the non-league and grassroots sectors.

There exists nowadays many other equality campaigning organisations and pressure groups with a specific focus on ending discrimination and championing support for equality in football for disabled people, women and girls and LGBTQ people. Others work to address anti-Semitism and tackle anti-Muslim prejudice and hatred. While Kick It Out seeks to be supportive on all fronts, it recognises that it is frequently better to work with others as they are often better placed, particularly at local level, to respond to problems where and when these arise. Occasionally, there has been a 'divide and rule' reaction from clubs and authorities. At times we have met resistance from clubs who may have had sessions presented to them by Show Racism the Red Card and would regard Kick It Out as duplication, even though the roles and activities are distinctly different. We would be admonished with: "We don't know the difference between Kick It Out and Show Racism the Red Card. Sort it out."

Community-based projects possess local knowledge and understand the needs of local people and are therefore well placed to assist football. But, they are excluded from doing so by institutionalised internal systems and processes in the game, which prefers to seek advisory inputs from professional and high-cost consultants rather than those in the knowledgeable voluntary sector with committed track records on equality. They are perceived wrongfully as unprofessional, but are low-cost or free, and are reliable and of equal value, especially in light of the many expensive failings of some of the biggest and 'best' business consultants. For instance, the FA and the Premier League would often seek independent expert input from the best professional consultants over and above the competence and capacity already in existence in community and voluntary organisations. The business side of football has to address the problems it faces and achieve equality and cohesion, and it would do well to utilise the help and guidance that is available from different voluntary sources.

Kick It Out has faced and overcome many challenges during its existence. The reality of its survival owed much to its staff and supporters, but moreover because racism, exclusion and discrimination still exists and is prevalent in football, as it is in many other parts of society. It remains institutionalised, notwithstanding the progress made to put equality up front as a priority. The human and societal traits of prejudice, ignorance, arrogance and complacency afflict us all in varying degrees, and football's decision-makers and other participants in the sport are not exempt. Of course, nowadays, there are excellent exemplars of good equality practice in football promoted by enlightened individuals who continue to challenge the system.

The initial campaign back in 1993 was to 'kick racism out of football'. The primary concern then was about the outrageous abuse, harassment and even violence showered on professional Black footballers on the field of play and also Black fans attending the matches. To that extent, the campaign could correctly and justifiably be claimed to have been successful. But in reality, that was then, and now the challenge is about the entirety of the whole game. Footballers entering the field of play today can expect the full protection from the authorities as the clubs offer better stewarding of the game and in the stadia; fans can complain about abuse and sometimes get action almost immediately; players who abuse others know they will be caught and punished appropriately and therefore refrain from doing so. Match day officials operate to a protocol to ensure that they have the authority to deal with any matter drawn to their attention that is abusive or discriminatory; and Kick It Out is heavily supporting clubs and their players with education and training on conduct and attitude matters in order to keep them on the right track of the rules and regulations.

Players and fans have also helped to achieve the position now reached. It has been a selfless slog for those who are at the frontline of the daily struggle for equality and inclusion in football. To think that after nearly three decades, the cries for help and action sound the same as they did back in 1993. Undoubtedly, the identifying of abuse, reporting it, having it investigated and dealt with in a proper manner and with the appropriate punishments, have been the cornerstones of the progress made to date. That must continue as other areas of less progress are prioritised. High profile cases such as those involving Chelsea's John Terry calling Queen's Park Rangers' Anton Ferdinand a "fucking black cunt"; Liverpool's Luis Suarez calling Manchester United's Patrice Evra a "negro"; and Eniola Aluko's complaints about her England team manager, Mark Sampsom's 'racist joke' being dismissed by the FA, received maximum publicity. This enabled action to be taken in order to achieve satisfactory outcomes and change practices and processes.

At the other end of the football pyramid, the FA must be congratulated for its Respect campaign, which is targeted at grassroots football. Over the past decade there has been considerable improvement in the conduct of families and friends of children and young people attending football matches involving children and youngsters. It is refreshing also to see the respect being shown to the referees, the other voluntary assisting officials and the numerous voluntary coaches. This has been a positive development and complements all the other activities taking place to help the next generation embrace the game as spectators, players and other participants in the right spirit and to show respect to others when doing so. But there remain ongoing problems, as evidenced by continuing disaffection at grassroots level about the failure of some of the county associations to deal with such complaints effectively and with fairness.

Kick It Out held a high priority for focusing on the grassroots sector. Its education and mentoring programmes were designed to equip those young people from all backgrounds with the confidence and knowledge to handle the stresses and adverse effects of racism, sexism, homophobia, disability discrimination, Islamophobia and other forms of discrimination. This is so crucial at a time when it is known that the decade of austerity has left many young people in some communities without youth clubs, outreach youth workers and community facilities and resources. This is also a time when extreme organisations and individuals are seeking to ramp up race and religious hatred, and football is often the only body providing effective and accessible community cohesion programmes for young people. It is now that football has to be seen, understood and appreciated as a potential powerhouse for good in building local community and social cohesion. The responsible leaders in the game have an important job to perform in this regard, and it is a vital one for football to undertake with increased resources and commitment, even more so in the current and post-Covid-19 crisis.

However, even with the better controls and surveillance now in place to deal with race hate abuse and all forms of unacceptable conduct at professional football clubs and venues, the expressions of hate persist. But for the past decade it has been moving onto the social media networks and platforms, where the trolls can peddle their venomous messages anonymously. Thankfully, the current and the next generation of footballers are showing signs that they will not leave any of this unchallenged, and want action to be taken by the authorities now. There is still the pathetic responses from the social media networks that they are doing all that they can, but that is all you get out of these billionaire entrepreneurs. They do not appear to have the will or courage to just do it. They have the technology, but they are spineless and uncaring about the suffering endured through vile hate messages on their platforms.

What is now most encouraging is the responsible leadership that is visible among the emergent generation of talented young Black players. Players such as Raheem Sterling, Tyrone Mings and Marcus Rashford are speaking out and speaking up. They are getting support from their fellow players and are demanding action to tackle all forms of hatred. They are not afraid to challenge the status quo and, at long last, there is a willingness to see the players take responsible leadership for themselves and the game as a whole. It is now up to the government and those in authority to deal with Twitter, Snapchat, Instagram, Facebook and YouTube, to put a stop to the irresponsible providers who for most of the past decade have allowed these hate-filled trolls to be abusive without recourse to justice.

FOURTEEN

Hostile environment

I n her early days as prime minister, Theresa May was scathing in her criticisms about people who appeared to lack patriotism because they considered themselves citizens of the world rather than citizens of the UK, describing them as, "Citizens of nowhere". But when people are told on the streets, at their workplaces and even in their homes that they do not belong, this is not your country and you are not wanted, how can they be proud and enthusiastic about feeling and being British or UK citizens? Her remarks may not have intended to inspire hatred of people who may not be overly patriotic or obviously "like us" in appearance, but language is important, especially coming from the leaders in society, such as the prime minister. Hate incidents, which have been on the rise annually, do not need to be encouraged, directly or indirectly, by the use of inappropriate language.

At the time of her speech, it was not envisaged that there was more substance to her views about some specific groups of people, which would later unravel spectacularly in 2018.

When she was home secretary, Theresa May had introduced the concept of the 'hostile environment.' She wanted to be known as tough on immigration and for getting rid of people in the UK who were deemed to be 'illegal'. The Home Office was a hotbed of problems for previous home secretaries and she was determined to be seen as tough, effective and successful in transforming the performance of a department of state described as, "Not fit for purpose". The hostile environment regime raised its ugly head in 2015 when the Home Office deployed a large bus to move around some neighbourhoods, with bold slogans urging people to leave the country immediately if they were illegally here, as otherwise they would be caught, arrested, imprisoned and deported. That initiative was thankfully disbanded following protests and outrage at this naked attempt to whip up a hatred of foreigners and demonstrate toughness.

Sometime before this, there had been newspaper reports about children of British citizens, who came to England from the Caribbean before 1973, now being classified as illegal. There had been little or no reaction from government and few, if any, expressions of concern. Yet some of these people were losing their homes as they were unable to work or receive benefits and were becoming destitute, whilst others were refused re-entry to the UK having left for a holiday or to visit relatives elsewhere. A number of people had even been detained in advance of their deportation. The hostile environment meant that some news outlets, far from expressing outrage at the inhuman treatment of people, took the view that the government was effectively doing its job of simply getting rid of people who should not be here. However, to others, the Home Office appeared to be a law onto itself, unaccountable, dismissive and disdainful and doing what the home secretary demanded. It had been getting away with such conduct for years and its priority was to rid the country of people to meet deportation targets and migration goals. Theresa May would have felt that she was on strong ground, being applauded by her colleagues in government and her supporters in the electorate and the media.

The circumstances of these cases had been drawn to the attention of Her Majesty's Government through official channels with representations made via the Foreign and Commonwealth Office as early as in 2013, but there was no recognisable nor sympathetic response. No one in government seemed to care, and certainly nothing happened to alleviate the growing concerns of many.

In February 2018, I was approached by the then high commissioner for Barbados, Guy Hewitt, seeking a meeting to discuss how the Caribbean high commissioners could contribute towards a resolution of this situation. In his view this was, "Causing considerable trauma and devastation to many affected families in the UK," who, having been settled as residents here for over 40 years, and having worked and paid their taxes, were now being told that they were here illegally. We met a few weeks later. For someone who is usually the epitome of calmness personified, Guy appeared considerably agitated because all efforts to date to draw attention to the hostile environment and the way people were being treated had failed. They were being made homeless, unemployed and unemployable, denied benefits, denied access to NHS treatment and, without money, could not pay their debts. They were told to go to the Home Office for advice and clarification on their status, but many refused to do so as they knew from other people's experiences that they would be immediately detained, if not able to prove their British citizenship and produce documentation covering every subsequent year of their pre-1973 residency in the country.

The Guardian newspaper was at the forefront of reporting cases where individuals had lost their homes and their jobs because they could not prove that they were British, even though they had lived in the UK for over fifty years and paid their taxes. Its regular daily reports exposed how individuals were being shown no mercy by Home Office officials who seemed not to be demonstrating any common sense or reasonableness. The paper's investigative reporter, Amelia Gentleman, was prolific and thorough in her award-winning coverage. Simon Israel at Channel 4 News was also alert and on the case. Satbir Singh at the Joint Council for the Welfare of Immigrants (JCWI) and some community based solicitors were also active in handling distressing cases, and Omar Khan at the Runnymede Trust was using his best endeavours to connect with parliamentarians and contacts in the Home Office and with other civil servants. The high commissioner sought support and advice from me and others to expose what was going on.

It was clear to me that the way forward required more of the same, but also urgent and intensive initiatives on three fronts. Firstly, publicity and exposure needed to be ramped up. Secondly, a focus on the forthcoming (April 2018) Commonwealth Heads of Government Conference, being hosted by the UK Government, with Her Majesty the Queen as head of the Commonwealth and Theresa May as prime minister at the helm. Thirdly, to get a prominent Member of Parliament to raise the matter in the Commons, generate support for a debate and for the prime minister to meet with the Caribbean Commonwealth heads of state. The Caribbean high commissioners, as diplomats, and their civil servants were cautious and wanted to steer clear of being regarded as entering the political arena, so it was unlikely that either the secretary general or the Commonwealth heads of government would want this matter brought up at their meeting in April.

Immediately after my meeting with the high commissioner I tabled six questions in the House of Lords for written answers from the government as follows:

1. What is their estimate of the number of people born in a Commonwealth country who have settled in the UK, having arrived before 1971, and who are now vulnerable to deportation as they have never regularised their status as UK citizens?
2. How many undocumented Commonwealth immigrants who were settled in the UK before 1971 have been deported in the past 24 months and to which countries?
3. What assessment have they made of the impact of deportation on the lives of those deported residents

who settled in the UK before 1971 but now find themselves effectively stateless?

4. What are the differences in processes to consider (i) undocumented Commonwealth Caribbean migrants settled in the UK before 1971 for removal, and (ii) EU citizens seeking permanent residence in the UK?

5. What steps they are taking to assist undocumented Commonwealth Caribbean migrants who settled in Britain before 1971 having arrived as British subjects on their parents' passports to regularise their status as British citizens?

The Home Office minister's answer on 26 March was a formal explanation of the provisions of the Immigration Act 1971 which came into effect in January 1973, the EU Free Movement Directive for EU citizens and the processes being applied by the Home Office. However, the minister's most significant answer was to my sixth question, which was:

"What representations they have received, including those from Commonwealth Caribbean countries, about children who arrived and settled in the UK before 1971 as British subjects on their parents' passports but are now being deported as undocumented illegal Commonwealth Caribbean migrants; and what were their responses?"

The Home Office minister's reply on 26 March was:

"We have not received any official representations from Commonwealth countries about their citizens who claim to be settled under the 1971 Act but have been subject to removal action."

This answer caused consternation among those high commissioners who were aware of the representations made in 2013. Over two months later, in June 2018, the minister issued a formal apology for providing misleading information in her reply and corrected her 26 March answer, having ascertained that the secretary of state for the Foreign and Commonwealth Office had indeed received representations. A genuine mistake? Perhaps. Or was this a case of one department not communicating with another? A cock-up or a cover-up?

As a result of the government's misinformation, it was felt that everything needed to be vigorously ramped up since it appeared that the Home Office had no qualms about distorting the truth in order to maintain the heat of their hostile environment for people for whom they had no care or concern. A formal press conference for interested sections of the media was held at the St Kitts and Nevis High Commission on 12th April, and several of the affected individuals, who were to become known as the Windrush Generation, shared their experiences. They talked about their life-long commitment to the UK and were distraught about the indifferent treatment and inhumanity shown to them by Home Office officials. The reality for those affected was that landlords were required to check if their tenants were legally in the UK, or otherwise would incur costly fines. Employers, too, had to seek such proof and, if it was not forthcoming, would have to get rid of long-standing employees or face similar consequences. Access to the NHS was also denied in some cases, especially for certain urgent procedures. Those deemed to be illegal were given as little as two weeks between detention and deportation to seek advice and legal representation. The individuals who told their stories at the press conference were understandably emotional, but were nevertheless convincing in their storytelling. Most of the Caribbean high commissioners attended the press conference and some contributed to the proceedings. This first part of "our" strategy was effective, with radio, television, newsprint and social media giving the matter extensive coverage. For its part the Home Office's formal position was:

"Those who have resided in the UK for an extended period but feel they may not have the correct documentation confirming their 'leave to remain' (residency) should take legal advice and submit the appropriate application with correct documentation so that we can progress the case. Where the Home Office requires evidence of a person's residency, the onus is on the applicant to be able to provide this proof."

In Parliament, David Lammy MP, Chair of the All Party Parliamentary Group on Race and Community, was incensed by the treatment of these long-standing residents and wasted no time in rounding up support to press for action by the government and the Home Office. He had recently found his distinctly powerful voice resonating to great effect, as he lambasted the government and the Royal Borough of Kensington and Chelsea about the tragic Grenfell Tower fire. Now he stunned the House of Commons with a passionate speech that heaped shame on the government about its disgraceful, inhumane treatment of the long-standing residents of the UK who were a part of the Windrush Generation. It had the immediate effect of bringing the issue not only to the attention of the British Parliament, but also the attention of the wider British public and beyond.

It was now the weekend before the Commonwealth Heads of Government conference. The Prime Minister was asked to meet with the Caribbean heads of government on this matter but the request was rejected, initially due to a busy PM's diary. However, once it was appreciated that the sting had to be taken out of this disastrous situation of disgraceful treatment of Commonwealth citizens by the country that was hosting the meeting, and with the Queen as head of the Commonwealth in attendance, the prime minister conveniently found an hour to meet the heads of government a day later.

On 23 April the Home Office issued a statement which acknowledged the devastating effect of its actions on the

Attending a meeting of Caribbean high commissioners, victims of the 'Windrush Scandal' and equality campaigners at the St Kitts and Nevis High Commission in London in April 2018. The meeting was convened to air their concerns about the impact of the British Government's Hostile Environment Policy and its effect on the status and treatment of Caribbean people who settled in the UK between the end of the Second World War and 1973 – the Windrush Generation. This meeting coincided with the Commonwealth Heads of Government Meeting also taking place in London.

people of the Windrush Generation, who had resided in the UK legally but who struggled to produce documentation to prove their status. However, it blamed their situation on the unintended consequences of the application of Home Office policies and procedures. In the light of all the unravelled unreasonable actions by the Home Office, the government immediately announced plans to waive a number of fees associated with applications for citizenship, irrespective of documentation, the Knowledge of Language and Life in the UK test, and cases where an application for naturalisation was necessary.

Those who had been refused re-entry to the UK during this period of the hostile environment could return and costs associated with this could possibly be waived. The Home Office set about resolving current cases and the then home secretary, Amber Rudd, set up a task force with the aim of achieving positive outcomes quickly to avoid further suffering among those affected. An inquiry and a compensation scheme were also proposed. Within days, however, Amber Rudd was forced to resign after failing to explain why she was unaware of the impact on people of the hostile environment and Home Office processes. She also, belatedly, admitted and confirmed that numerical targets were driving the department's enthusiasm for defining people as illegal, something she had previously denied.

The new home secretary, Sajid Javid, rushed into office with a pledge to reform the Home Office and put right all the wrongs associated with the hostile environment which he intended to discard and substitute with a "compliant environment".

In an answer to a subsequent parliamentary question by the Green Party's MP, Caroline Lucas, it also transpired that the government had not acted on the recommendations of a 2014 report that had highlighted the problems faced by older, long-term UK residents who had no documents. The 'Chasing Status Report', produced when Theresa May was home secretary, had urged that a unit be set up to fast-track cases of people who lived in the UK before 1973 and ensure they enjoyed the full rights and entitlements of British citizenship. If that had been implemented, this would have averted this disaster of deporting British citizens.

So much for unintended consequences – no attention had been given to representations made to government more than five years earlier, and now the situation had blown-up spectacularly in its face. For many people, it appeared to be the usual shameful and utter contempt for justice and fair treatment for the Windrush Generation, and a complete failure to act humanely. Unintended consequences arise from institutionalised discriminatory cultures and methods. Of course, the victims, the Windrush Generation from the Caribbean, are overwhelmingly Black. If this fiasco was not another classic example of institutional racism and discrimination, then it was clearly a case of straightforward and deliberate racial discrimination. But who cared? The previous home secretary was gone, and her successor decided he would put matters right with what he now called a 'compliant environment'.

It was felt that, if he genuinely understood how institutional racism exists and how it should be tackled, there was hope for the future, and we watched and waited before making judgement. He made excellent powerful statements and instituted some actions, but he eventually moved on from the Home Office to the Treasury. It was not much later during 2018 when Diane Abbott and David Lammy revealed that the Home Office had already reneged on some commitments in relation to compensation, and was imposing non-disclosure confidentiality agreements on those who did receive payments. An independent fact-finding review of the whole fiasco revealed aspects of institutional racism in the Home Office administration. Moving forward, it was disgraceful that in 2020, as the coronavirus pandemic ripped through the country, many of the Windrush Generation who were the victims of discriminatory and detrimental treatment were still waiting for the justice promised. Four home secretaries – Theresa May, Amber Rudd, Sajid Javid and Priti Patel – were all tarnished by this fiasco. The first created the hostile environment; the second offered excuses to minimise the extent and reality of abuses; the third and current one pledged to resolve the grievances and compensate for detriments inflicted which are still outstanding in 2021.

FIFTEEN

Responsible leadership

Throughout the entirety of my working life, at all levels and different spheres of activities, I have learnt to admire and trust those people who demonstrate moral values of fairness and are prepared to practice what they preach. They also have a genuine sense of the power they hold and how to use that to help achieve equality and fair treatment without prejudice, bias or fear, and to influence others to do likewise. Responsible leadership and positive action can generate optimism, improve trust and inspire confidence among people where there is an imperative to implement policies in pursuit of equality. When applied with thorough commitment, there is certainty of achieving tangible and measurable results with the inevitable benefits for those who are usually excluded and denied access to opportunities to improve their quality of life and play a fuller part in society. There is a substantive body of evidence to justify the benefits of sustainable best equality practices leading to beneficial outcomes for employers, employees, public and commercial services.

My own experiences in several sectors of society reaffirm such a conclusion. By way of example I shall focus on one sector in British society: football in England. Although only one particular section of society, I believe that many of the issues identified have relevance for the whole nation, showing what not to do and also some ways that point to the success of positive initiatives, yielding important results for race and community relations in Britain. Racism and discrimination, as previously discussed, have infected football, its operations, its power and decision-making business structures, and highlighted its failures to respond to inequalities and to exclusion. After decades of being in denial, it may now be benefiting from the example of emergent responsible leadership from a handful at those of the top of the football business.

Putting to one side the effects of the on-going covid pandemic, football has mass public participation, extensive publicity and coverage and considerable financial inward investment, while making a huge contribution to the Treasury's coffers and a considerable emotional impact on people's lives. In 2018, The Football Association estimated that the game had more than 11 million participants, 30 million spectators and 90,000 grassroots teams. It set out its stall in pursuit of the benefits the sport and the nation can derive by embracing the principles and objectives required to achieve equality, diversity and inclusion in all its activities, and to make football a sport that is accessible to all people.

The FA got a taste of what could be achieved through the experiences from the FIFA 2018 World Cup tournament in Russia. Russia proved to be an excellent host and ran the event efficiently and with an emphasis on safety and security for fans from thirty-one other countries, averting any of the predicted violence from local racist and homophobic 'ultras'. What was truly remarkable was how fans from all backgrounds celebrated the joys of the game, having travelled to Russia in their thousands from countries like Australia, Japan, Colombia, Uruguay and Argentina. They shared their own and others' cultures inside and outside the stadia, made new friends and were welcomed by local families in the towns and neighbourhoods wherever they were located with their countries' teams. Also remarkable was the impact made by the England contingent, a squad of players that reflected the country's multicultural and multi-ethnic characteristics, led by a team manager, Gareth Southgate, who used his skill, charm and humility to bring his players close to the fans and vice-versa. The performances were also better than expected, which had fans purring with anticipation that England could get to the final for the first time since 1966 (although it was not to be, with Croatia knocking England out in the semi-final).

We saw men and women, boys and girls, those of all faiths and none, disabled people, people of all ethnic backgrounds and different sexual orientations, all mixing. Together they shared moments of hope, elation, frustration and disappointment, as thirty million people watched the England semi-final match on screens all over this country. It was a glimpse of the power football has to bring people together, share emotional moments in support of the national team and be proud of the players of different heritages, backgrounds and circumstances who, clearly, were proud to represent their country. For a moment it looked as though football could, at last, help to solve some of the race relations and inequalities problems, but reality soon kicked in. The 2018/19 season was about to start and racial abuse was already evident in the pre-season 'friendlies', a trend still to be challenged.

If the football industry is to become a 'powerhouse for cohesion', that generates best practice in equality in England, it will require responsible, imaginative, and bold leadership. There is some emergent evidence of these qualities at the top of the game in England, but it is spread thinly across different parts of the sport which remains inhibited by traditional attitudes such as: "We like to do things our way," and, "We don't like telling others what to do," as well as, "We don't like others telling us what to do."

It is a reality of English football that bodies such as The FA, the Premier League, the English Football League, the League Managers' Association, the Professional Footballers Association, the professional clubs and many others are each independent entities. They do work together, very successfully, in most cases. But my twenty-six years of experience while leading Kick It Out in trying to get the whole of football to work collegiately, to share information, especially equality data, and co-ordinate strategies was a monumental, uphill task. There have been small successes over those two and half decades to note, with some achievements to applaud, but also many disappointments that arouse disillusionment.

I had always regarded the FA as the body to take the lead on such matters, and to set the standards on equality and inclusion. When called upon in 2018 to seize the moment and step up, its reaction was that, "We have to put our own house in order with our equality, inclusion and cohesion policies and achievements before we tell others what to do." Whilst that was a sensible approach, it also reflected a mentality that constrains the sharing of knowledge and experiences. It limits the utilisation of expertise in different organisations that could help to optimise the use of skills that exist across the game and avoid reinventing the wheel too often. For instance, even in a small charitable organisation like Kick It Out, there are individuals, including myself when I was there, with a range of skills which are, more often than not, overlooked by the various bodies. Their preference is usually to buy-in advice from established, external management consultants. This is not unique. It was also a constant feature in many of my previous employment experiences and scenarios. External management consultants would turn up, pick your brain and write up whatever they got from you and others, generously padded with expansive narrative, glamorously packaged and professionally presented. Job done!

Kick It Out's offer would be regarded as inferior because it came, to an extent, free of charge and without the private sector badge of approval. It came with an emphasis on action and outcomes. Their preferred option comprised more theory and modelling, with recommendations made by people who would have had little or no hands on experience, but had succeeded in plotting their way along higher education pathways into lucrative consultancy positions. The use of such external organisations, with their specialists, is vital in supporting changes in organisations, but it remains a grievance, as expressed in the question: "Why always them and very rarely us?"

The necessity of stressing this scenario yet again is because responsible leadership should also not overlook the talent and opportunities staring them in the face. It is often the people who they walk past on a regular basis who can make effective and useful contributions, but are often disregarded as irrelevant.

The need for responsible, co-ordinated leadership to steer football toward becoming one of the best led sport industries in England for equality is an issue that cannot be avoided just because every league, club, The FA and others are independent business entities. Each of them is doing good work but in different ways, at their own pace and with differential impact. Professional football clubs are more inclined to steer a course without external influence, although they have to comply with rules and regulations enforced by The FA and leagues, which they, in part, helped to draw up, including on equalities. A more inclusive and coherent approach (not just good intentions) is needed to achieve equality outcomes, and this means demonstrable leadership and effective coordination across the game.

One area of considerable activity by football clubs which is worthy of considerable praise is the work done in the community. Most football organisations can appear to have a tendency to be inward looking and act in their own self-interest. But they are also often ready and willing to fulfil their corporate social responsibility obligations beyond merely tokenistic contributions.

For five years I served as a trustee of the Manchester United Foundation so I am aware of how much the football club, as a separate entity, supported the charitable body in generating funds. These not only benefitted local community trusts, schools and care institutions, but also assisted development work in other parts of the world through its partnership with UNICEF. The local work focused on schools, a girls' football centre of excellence, health and well-being initiatives, mentoring, diversity and education programmes, as well as football in the community projects for young people of all backgrounds, including those with disabilities and special needs. Virtually all of the other professional clubs are similarly active in reaching out and involving their local communities with initiatives and activities which bring benefits to children, young people and adults from all backgrounds. This work is vital to promoting community cohesion through mixing and relationship-building between individuals from different multicultural, faith, ethnic and social-class backgrounds; it also contributes to social mobility and community cohesion. There have been many commendable actions by clubs, their staff, players and fans in support of starving children and vulnerable individuals during the Covid-19 virus health emergency.

The FA is striving to become a modern 21st century governing body and a leader of change by putting its own house in order, following many setbacks. In its Equality, Diversity and Inclusion Plan, former Chairman Greg Clarke talked about the role of football in society:

"From Boardroom to boot-room, we can lead change. Football shouldn't just be trying to keep up with the pace of societal change, it should be leading."

He was clear about how football could help to normalise conversations on LGBTQ issues and remove stigma when it comes to mental health. He was also clear that, while the FA has to be responsible and accountable for equality, diversity and inclusion achievements in those areas of the game over which it has control, it must also continue to work with the other football authorities to diversify the football landscape. This sounds like positive and committed leadership. Most leaders who succeed in the implementation of positive equality programmes do so because they take ownership and make things happen – otherwise it won't. When working on organisational change I always asked individual leaders if they knew what their performance was on equality and inclusion matters. They would often look elsewhere in their organisations for the answers, expecting others rather than themselves to be accountable for this. If they are not interested, it shows, and if they don't know what their performance on equality is, then it is likely that implementation is not happening and planned outcomes will not be achieved. That is a reality.

Legislation since the turn of the millennium has coupled human rights protections with equality considerations, so that the characteristics of faith and belief, age, sexuality, gender, disability and race have the same legal protection from discrimination. But challenging inequalities in society is more than just race, sex and disability discrimination, although these have often been the main focus of attention. One of the most important characteristics of inequality is poverty. You do not have to be poor to be discriminated against, but the poor are more likely to be excluded, disadvantaged and deprived in ways that leave them vulnerable to discriminatory outcomes in all aspects of their lives. Economic disadvantage and social class discrimination restrict life chances and trap low income families in increasing debt while they try to keep the bailiffs at bay. It restricts social mobility and limits opportunities to escape the revolving door of multiple deprivations.

The Blair government, when elected, was committed to ending poverty and improving social mobility. It had the aim of giving children the best start in life and was underpinned by the Sure-Start programme of nursery education and care provision. This investment yielded good results but was short-lived, as the subsequent Coalition and Conservative governments from 2010 presided over the demise of the programme, adversely affecting pre-school advances for children with particular needs and their stressed families.

By 2018, and subsequently, it was evident that society was becoming more polarised due to inequalities, including many households where the adults are in work but are earning insufficient income and are not effectively or adequately supported by state benefits. Mental health issues (including among children), the care of the elderly or those with physical disabilities and the lack of accessible and affordable housing were serious causes for concern, but insufficient resources were available to meet these needs. Income inequality affects all ethnic groups, but those who are vulnerable to multiple discrimination feel its adverse impacts disproportionately, and the gap between rich and poor continues to widen. Too many vulnerable families and individuals experiencing income deprivation have become reliant on food banks for family sustenance, and are deprived of equality of opportunity in education, health care and housing. All these are contributing to the divisiveness we are now seeing in communities around the country, as a consequence of the politics associated with attitudes to immigration, the hatred expressed towards some faith groups and the existence of extremist organisations that promote hate. These circumstances can only change if responsible leadership articulates the justifiable need for equality to the electorate, and leads the way in government to deliver the essential actions to achieve a just and fair society for all people.

SIXTEEN

A just society for all

I n recent times, a recurrent mantra for leading politicians has been, "We are all in this together." Sometimes, such as the support for the NHS during the national emergency in 2020, there is scope to be optimistic of a society in which we treat each other with dignity and respect and care for each other. Other times, such as the evidence of the effects of the disproportionality experienced by poor and vulnerable communities, the country is socially, politically, economically and culturally divided. There is speculation about the concept of the 'new normal' as opposed to what has gone before the global coronavirus pandemic. But, it is premature to expect that our society will suddenly reflect all the values and joys of fairness, equality and justice for all the people of the UK. Any post-covid economic recession could result in hardship, deprivation and potential for a new blame culture targeting certain groups. Political leadership of the highest quality will be essential to maintain consensus of human values and hang on to the commitment of fair treatment for all.

It cannot be taken for granted that disgruntled communities will not take to the streets as they have before when forced between a rock and a hard place and with no scope for escape. Previous experience over recent decades confirms that people do not riot because they are poor; but they will not hold back forever when they are harshly and disproportionately policed and looked down upon as a result of ignorance, hatred and snobbery. When discussions about integrated communities are under the spotlight, they are usually about racial and religious integration. The wealthy, with their gated mansions and extra security, are kept far away from those who are regarded as 'undesirable', too poor in wealth, culture and status to share in their space. White communities living with their own and in their own confines are never regarded as being segregated. On the other hand, Black, Asian and other minority groups who live close to each other are criticised for being reluctant to integrate.

During the past two decades, debates about integration, segregation, identity and Britishness have taken us back to the fundamental issue of inequalities along race, sex and social class lines. There is reluctance in such debates to focus on the more contentious and complex realities about who makes the decisions, controls the resources and who are conscious of the need for moral and responsible leadership to take decisive actions for fair and just outcomes. We might all appear to be in the same boat when the value of the pound decreases, inflation increases, food and fuel prices rise and debt interest charges increase, but we are on different decks when it comes to how we will be able to cope. We are not all in this together, as some politicians and leaders claim.

Try experiencing the multiple discrimination which some groups of people have to contend with. You can cushion your loss in real terms if you are well off and able to make ends meet, but there are increasing numbers of households and families where this is not an option. They cannot reduce their debt or keep the bailiffs away; they must look to food banks for support and cannot shrug off the shame and stigma of poverty. Some observers argue that such impoverished conditions breed fear and resentment within white communities who blame Black, Asian and other minority ethnic communities, whether newcomers or born here, for the problems they face. In my experience there is a shared reality of 'them and us' within deprived communities for whom there should be empathy and support. When people are assisted to overcome their fears misperceptions and irrational racial and religious prejudices they are more inclined to mix with and learn from others about their different realities. They begin to see themselves on a more level playing field, notwithstanding differences in ethnicity, faith, skin colour, culture or language.

Most people aspire to improve their and their family's quality of life and, not surprisingly, feel more comfortable living alongside other people of similar culture. That is an understandable human trait that cannot, nor should be completely resisted. Others, however, seek to improve their lot by escaping from what they may see as a humdrum existence and are relaxed about living in more mixed ethnic and multicultural communities.

Increased social interaction between different communities living in mixed ethnic neighbourhoods and sharing space in the workplace and elsewhere have helped to dispel some of the fears and misperceptions that are created by ignorance and disinformation. Prejudice, ignorance and hatred are not the preserve of any single racial or ethnic group, and we all benefit from knowing more about each other through mixing, learning and sharing. Yet some commentators and leaders still assert that 'multiculturalism' is to blame for the ills of race and religious tensions in Britain today. Those influential leaders talk about British standards, values, language and national heritage and the need for these to be shared by all those who live in the UK. They argue that, if there is to be community cohesion, there must be a recognition that other cultures and national loyalties cannot have equal status alongside British values, rights, standards and jurisdiction. Those who assert the rights of minorities to express themselves in ways that reflect their cultures and faiths are identified as the high priests and priestesses of multiculturalism who create divisiveness and encourage segregation.

Campaigns against 'political correctness' and so-called 'multiculturalism' have been prevalent since the speeches of Enoch Powell in 1968 and Margaret Thatcher in 1978. Racial and social integration were never serious and sustainable political priorities that were translated into meaningful programmes to deal with inequalities, transform deprived areas, promote social mobility and tackle prejudice in all communities. Social and racial integration cannot happen on unequal terms, and the failure to end inequalities and injustice across all ethnic groups and social classes is at the heart of the current crisis and the focus on identity, Britishness, Englishness and the negative perceptions of cultural diversity.

Cultural diversity flourishes when people from different backgrounds unite in the struggle to eliminate racial discrimination and when people from different ethnic groups, faiths and other characteristics are encouraged to learn together and respect each other's cultures and lifestyles. Multiculturalism, as a concept, is only meaningful if it is underpinned by anti-racism and equality policies and programmes for which there is genuine strong and moral political leadership. The campaigns apportioning blame on political correctness and multiculturalism for devaluing British standards and values, and undermining national identity, are clearly diversionary. They seem designed to remove any blame from those who are responsible for the failure to provide the responsible leadership necessary to tackle and eliminate racism, sexism, anti-Semitism, homophobia, Islamophobia, disability discrimination and economic inequalities.

A priority for the future of community cohesion in multicultural Britain must be to build trust and confidence in the next generation through all the basic formal education programmes. The increasing ethnic and cultural diversity in the population provides the opportunity for all children's education to incorporate an honest awareness about Britain's multi-racial history, its role when the British Empire was dominant, and the realities of 21st century Britain. It is of fundamental importance that the country's leaders ensure that our children are educated about prejudice, bigotry, xenophobia, antisemitism, discrimination and the effects of hatred, and that this is underpinned by sustainable initiatives to tackle and end inequalities.

In the post-Brexit and post-pandemic era, a primary goal must be to take action and introduce initiatives that will heal divisions between people and in different communities, and to bring about greater community cohesion. Examples of positive community cohesion should be highlighted, supported and consolidated, with lessons learned and shared about initiatives which have resulted in successful representation. Having open and effective decision-making which reflects the characteristics of a local neighbourhood's population will lead to greater inclusion, inspiring trust and confidence in leaders and decision making. This will require responsible leadership from central and local government and all sectors in society, including business, finance, culture, health, housing, education, the environment, the arts, communities and faith.

At different times I have found inspiration in hearing from some leaders who embody a passion for equality, fairness and justice, and want to show the way ahead. In this context, I would make mention of the different inspirational faith leaders who tirelessly strive to work collaboratively, celebrating diversity and demonstrating unity across all faiths and none. Their moral stance and standard-setting encourages joint work that brings people from all backgrounds together, which is beneficial for Britain and an example of responsible leadership at work. They may not always be right and their views not necessarily always acceptable, but they are sincerely motivated in doing good for all, are influential, have millions of followers across all faiths and their approach is a positive example of 'British values' in action. This is the concept that many politicians and leaders, as well as critics of our multi-dimensional society, use as the flagship for promoting 'Britishness'.

There will continue to be many questions about what 'Britishness' really is, and whether there should be a national identity associated with being English in the same way as is enjoyed by the Scots, Welsh and Irish. People of dual heritage, including those who were born here as well as non-white British citizens who have come to this country from around the world, are challenged about their loyalty and commitment to Great Britain or the UK. Where do different faiths and ethnicities fit into the British or the devolved nations' identities? Who are you? Who am I? Who are we? What are we? Does 'us' include all of us, whatever our appearance, circumstances and characteristics? Is this 'our' country and are we all part of 'our'?

There are double standards and hypocrisy in our prejudices and stereotypes which enables us to perceive and treat some people as good, others as great and others as bloody awful. More subtle, is how we make these distinctions. Social media, while offering so many communication and learning benefits, has enabled some people to peddle their hatred and bile. I am always mindful of my experience in the 1970s, working in the care sector managing elderly people's residential facilities. The residents were 99 per cent white, the care staff were 70 per cent white, mostly Irish, and the domestic staff were predominantly Black. On several occasions, when residents did not want to be "touched by a darkie", they would follow up with, "... although I have nothing against them." Over time, when such 'touching' was necessary for their essential care, the narrative changed to, "You're all right, my dear, it's all the others I don't like."

Nowadays there is a different reality, and our elderly population is desperate for assurances that they will receive any care at all. As long as it is good it will not matter who is providing it. A more relatively recent example to demonstrate the double standards which exist in how we see and treat people can be drawn from the world of sport. The German footballer, Mesut Ozil (of Turkish heritage), up until recently, played for Arsenal football club in London. He accused the German Football Association of racism because they blamed him for the team's failure in the 2018 World Cup. He said that whenever they won, he was regarded as German, but when they lost, he was described as Turkish. He said he would no longer play for Germany.

Other high-profile sporting personalities have had similar experiences. When they are successful they are British or English but if they do not live up to expectations they are sometimes identified with the countries of their heritage, even if they were born here. In the early days of Kick It Out, a successful Premier League, England international Black footballer talked about how he and his family were abused on the street. His reality was: "On the pitch I am a hero; on the street I am just another nigger!" This, however, is the unholy reality faced by many Black players that draws from the well of bigotry and ignorance.

The diversity challenge is a conundrum for everyone and the circle has to be squared urgently. Our different realities should not mean that people believe they will receive unfavourable and unfair treatment because of who they are. The inherent challenge is to build trust and confidence within all communities that inequalities can and will be tackled. Responsible, bold, imaginative and persuasive leadership can take this agenda forward.

Britain has a deserved reputation as a nation of people who value freedom, fairness, democracy, tolerance and decency, underpinned by a commitment to protect human and civil rights. However, the reality is that inequalities exist in our society that deny individuals and vulnerable groups of people the opportunity to enjoy the benefits of such cherished values. A coherent society, at ease with itself and striving for equality justice and fair treatment, requires responsible leadership, both individual and collective, to inspire the nation to accept the sacrifices we all must make, to achieve the goal of a fair and just society. A dream, or an achievable goal?

One example, from my varied experience of observing institutional change, and adjusting to diversity, is the House of Lords. That will come as a surprise to many people. The House of Lords is widely regarded as a place of privilege, honour and an exclusive club. Although I find it embarrassing to be described as a Lord or Baron, it is an adjustment I had to make in order to enjoy having a seat on the red benches in parliament. My own experience there has been educational, valuable and enlightening. It is a place where integrity nobly thrives, and is full of fascination, intrigue and contrasts.

Its fundamental functions are law-making and holding the government to account on actions and policies, which it undertakes with thoroughness and careful scrutiny. Although there are divisions along party lines, there are also independent members, much coalescing and the personal honour that each member brings as part of their public service contribution. Most members are leaders of some sort, as most have achieved much already in their lives and are experts in specific areas of business, their chosen profession, charitable activities and public services.

They were, and still are, mainly men, but transformation has been taking place over recent decades. Women peers now take centre stage and their presence, due to their leadership qualities, personalities and immense public service commitments, have driven the cultural change. Those male members who were resistant to change because of their commitment to history and tradition have mostly been totally won over, even though a few might sulk quietly. Disabled people, minority ethnic members, and other minority groups are also now visible, irrespective of sexual orientation, religion, faith or cultural background.

The House of Lords nowadays embraces diversity and inclusion but is still disproportionately a bastion of white male privilege. However, its main critics want it abolished or reformed because none of its members have been democratically elected by the public in the way that members of parliament in the House of Commons are elected. The Peers' legitimacy to be law makers continues to be challenged on that basis. There is no political consensus to support any particular model for a revised second chamber that would overcome all the objections and shortcomings which now exist. But, the leading members of the Lords are committed to reform. They accept that the House is overpopulated, have been encouraging members to retire (I agreed, retired and left in May 2019) and are trying to persuade government to limit dramatically any essential future political appointments. This is not proving to be successful when considering the number of political nominees coming from the leaders of the main political parties.

There is also a tightening up of regulatory activities and closer enforcement of the code of conduct which sets out the standards of conduct expected by members of the House of Lords in the discharge of their parliamentary duties.

Compared to the House of Commons, the Lords' proceedings are conducted on a self-regulatory basis and there is a commitment to allow others to air their views. Because there are so many 'great' individuals who possess considerable expertise and achievements, I was in awe of the institution when I arrived there in 2001. One of my earliest experiences of what would be in store over the ensuing years took place during a debate about 'same race adoption and fostering of children in care'. I approached the debate with confidence and assuredness about my own position on the subject and my reasons for holding my views. I was soon changing my mind, having heard one convincing speech followed by another made by members. I was somewhat bewildered by this new experience. It was a reality check for me that powerful opposing arguments, with justification, were made to be listened to with care and

With my mother, Daphne, at the House of Lords in June 2001 when
I was introduced by Lords Navnit Dholakia and Brian Rix.

attention, and it was neither weakness nor inadequacy to form a different view after hearing the arguments, even though I was confident about my own strong views on the subject.

Having an open mind is an advantage, I feel, when seeking to argue for change. When I first entered the House of Lords, I firmly held the view that its replacement should be a totally elected second chamber, which is a view I no longer hold. The change has come about by listening and learning and benefiting from the range of wisdom being shared by those with vast experience. It requires reform to be smaller in its composition, as a working second chamber, to support the effective governance of the country by working with the government of the day and holding it to account without having the power to frustrate the wishes of elected House of Commons. But, there is no one option of what the second chamber should be that captures majority support among the members of the Commons and the Lords.

My time in the Lords has been consumed with numerous requests made by individuals who have seen me as a last resort for helping them to resolve difficult matters, where they, mistakenly, believe I have extra power or ability to do so. Alas, I found to my astonishment, I have had as much difficulty as them in getting answers from government ministers or their departments over the years. Equally, I have invested much time in putting down questions for written answers, most of which are anodyne and unenlightening, although in recent years have got much better. Visiting schools and talking about the work of the House of Lords and my professional career in local government, as well as charitable work and campaigning on equality matters, continued to dominate my life while present as a member of the House of Lords.

In citing the visible changes in parliament over the past two decades, I am not putting forward the House of Lords as an institution that is an exemplar of diversity, inclusion and cohesion. What I have observed in person, prior to my retirement in 2019, is a place full of people who have exercised degrees of responsible leadership. They have witnessed, endured and even welcomed recent dramatic changes to their House that now demonstrates that people from all backgrounds can play their parts as equals in the democratic processes and governance of the country, when such opportunities are opened up to all. We are still very far away from the end of the journey but the benefits from equality are already clear. Some people choose not to consider the future, and continue to live in their own blinkered reality. I, on the other hand, have moved on. Everyone should know when their time is up. I am no visionary, and my own reality is that I am in the final phase of my life and must determine the best path ahead for me.

SEVENTEEN

Back to oblivion

After fifty-six years of public, voluntary and charitable service, I increasingly found my energy levels low, with rapidly diminishing enthusiasm for never-ending conflict and confrontation, as well as declining personal health and well-being. It was clear to me as long ago as 2012 that I may be 'past my sell-by date' and should have been looking to wind down my ongoing and never ending activities, and devote more of my time to my family. With a chronic back ailment and other emergent health afflictions, mostly due to the ageing processes and sporting exploits in my youth, I now know that I should have headed for the hills a decade ago!

Nearly twenty years ago, I promised my family to pack up working full time when I reached my 55th birthday in the year 2000. That anticipated, and often re-adjusted, milestone of retirement came and went over and over. I did feel bad, but always, with hindsight, wrongly prioritised my public service commitments to others over and above my domestic responsibilities.

Despite the dereliction of my family duties, my personal efforts to improve local government and community relations have not gone entirely unnoticed, and I was publicly rewarded with a Knighthood in 1997 before I was made a life peer in 2001. I have also been awarded fourteen honorary degrees from universities from Edinburgh to Brighton, and in 2020 was delighted to receive the Pride of Britain Award which was presented to me by Viv Anderson, the first Black footballer to play for England. I was truly astonished to receive this particular award and to have it presented to me at the very club – Dulwich Hamlet FC – where I used to play as a youngster.

It seems that there was never a moment in this millennium when there was any let up in the demands on my time every day of the week, making it seemingly impossible to walk away from my charitable activities such as being the chairperson of Kick It Out or the Chandran Foundation. I loved the foundation, especially working with the much admired and respected Captain Chandran. From around 2010, I was keen to step down from Kick It Out. I was convinced that the football authorities would continue in their lethargy to embrace the necessary action to tackle the endemic institutional discrimination rooted in the cultural and organisational structures of the different governing bodies. No one at Kick It Out wanted to take the baton from me, but now they have realised that someone else would have to step forward.

There comes a time when enough is enough. The end is nigh, as they say. I gave notice to the House of Lords of my intention to retire and leave the House. My frustrations with colleagues at Kick It Out and some of those at the top of the football organisations convinced me that it was now time to walk away from them as well.

However, before doing so, there was a moment when I publicly called out the leadership following the Chelsea versus Manchester City match at Stamford Bridge in December 2018, when Raheem Sterling, the Black Manchester City and England international player, was racially abused. I witnessed the incident on television, and was astonished that Raheem did not react, and I admired his dignity and composure in the face of such abuse. The next day he gave his view via social media about the abuse he received. He considered that media bias played a role in fuelling racist attitudes and contributed to the hateful abuse inflicted on him when he plays for both club and country.

My view was simple, and proved to be both controversial and also a wake-up call. When asked what should have happened, I responded with mild rage that it should not have been left to Raheem to have to tell his story. Those who had a responsibility to intervene at the time of the incident appeared to do little or nothing.

I said: "Where was the FA? Where was the Premier League? Where was his employer? Where was his trade union, the PFA? Where was Chelsea Football Club, whose fans were the abusers? And why always come to Kick It Out for a reaction? Where are the leaders of these bodies and why no action? What are they waiting for?"

My reaction appeared to strike at the heart of the matter! I had a call from the chairman of Chelsea Football Club, Bruce Buck, someone who I greatly admire and respect. I was aware of how much his club was trying to do regarding such matters and appreciated his irritation. The outgoing executive chairman of the Premier League, Richard Scudamore, wrote an article in the press highlighting the many excellent programmes which the Premier League was doing. The chairman of the Football Association, Greg Clarke, expressed to me his determination to go after the people who were hell bent on inflicting such awful abuses at football matches in England. We wait, we watch and we hope for a turnaround.

Yet at the beginning of 2019, there were still reports of homophobic, racist, sexist and anti-Semitic abuses, an indication of what may be in store for the future without the necessary co-ordinated action required by the leadership across the entirety of the football establishment in England.

I cannot fail to praise and commend Bruce Buck at Chelsea, who wasted no time in talking to fans directly, and issuing immediate bans to those found to have perpetrated such abuses. He is the model of what

responsible leadership in football should be. He is also well
supported by his club's owner, Roman Abramovich, who does
not publicly say much, but his commitment to equality are
second to none in football.

Now, the reality of what, in my view, should have
happened when Raheem Sterling was being abused was
quite simply this: Sterling could possibly have told the
referee what had happened to him. There is protocol to
enable all players to do so and have appropriate action
taken. He and his captain should have asked the referee to
get the stadium administrators to deal with the matter
forthwith, by identifying the perpetrators and removing
them and making an announcement. They were clearly
identifiable. I would have expected the chairman of Chelsea
or others at the club to take immediate action. Undoubtedly
they took action behind the scenes but no-one knew of that!
I would have expected the Manchester City directors sitting
in their very comfortable seats in the stadium to have been
jumping up and down with rage that one of their star
players, who they were paying an alleged £300,000 weekly
wage for his service, was being abused and receiving no
protection. I would have expected both the FA and Premier
League to have initiated immediate investigations.

The reality is even simpler. When the campaign 'Kick
Racism out of Football' was initiated in 1993, I held the
view, which I know was shared by many fair-minded people,
that the players should not have to tolerate the incessant
abuse of Black players, and their union should withdraw
their services until it was sorted. By contrast with the
incident at Chelsea, a few weeks later there was a similar
incident in Italy. The then Napoli football club manager,
Carlos Ancelotti, told the football authorities in Italy that
he will take his players off the pitch the next time any of
his players are racially abused if they are not protected. He
is to be admired. But, why is it always the next time? The
next time nearly always needs yet another next time. Why
did he not take them off on this occasion?

For me there is no next time. It is now. For me, that means heading for the hills, caring for family and friends, finding some solace in the final phase of life and aspiring to belong to a community of communities in which there is no tolerance for ignorance, prejudice, hatred, abuse and discrimination.

INDEX OF NAMES

9/11 attacks, 2001 146

Abbott, Diane 177
Abramovich, Roman 161, 201
Abrams, Joe 106
Ali, Mohammed, QED 128
All Party Parliamentary Group on
  Race and Community 174
Alleyns Public School 38
Allied forces, African, Asian and
  Caribbean contribution to
  during the two world wars 22
Aluko, Eniola 157, 165
Amos, Valerie 64
Ancelotti, Carlos 201
Anderson, Viv 199
Armed Forces 123, 127
Armed Services 124, 125, 127
Arnie 38
Arsenal Football Club 152, 159,
  161, 192
Arts Committee 74
Atkinson, Ron 161
Atlantic Road, Brixton 51
Audit Commission 150
Ayling, Robert 112, *129*

Bahl, Kamlesh 109
Bailey, Vic 34
Baker, Kenneth 88
Baldrey, John 33
Bank of England 112, 123, 128
Banks, Tony 74
Barnfield, Robin 23
Batson, Brendon 154
BBC 128

Bean, Gerlin 46
Bellos, Linda 81
Benefits Agency 106
Bermondsey, south London 9
Bernstein, David 156
Berry, George 46
Better English Company 128
Bhalla, Anita 128
Big Society 146
Birdie (aunt) 19, 21
Black Lives Matter movement 15
Black Prince pub, Kent 33
Black Watch soldiers 8
Blair, Tony, Prime Minister 14, 78,
  115, 120, 122, 129, 147, 184
Bland, John 36, 40, 43
Blissett, Luther 154
Board of Jewish Deputies 128
Boateng, Paul 70, 129
Boreland-Kelly, Lorna 88
Bottomley, Peter 107
Bradford Breakthrough 137
Bradford Chamber of Commerce 137
Bradford College 137
Bradford Council 137
Bradford Health Authorities 137
Bradford Metropolitan Borough
  Council 136
Bradford University 137
Bradford Vision 137
Brexit 147, 190
Bristol REC 128
British Airways 112, *129*
British Empire 9, 189
British Fascist Movement 22
British Guiana (Guyana) 8, 19-21

British Movement 45
Brixton Neighbourhood
    Community Association 46
Brixton riots, 1981 50, 139
Brixton Road 49
Brixton, south London 44, 46-51,
    128, *129*, 139
Bromley Council 67
Brooks, Duwayne 107
Brown, Gordon 120, 122, 129
Buck, Bruce 161, 200
Business in the Community 112, *129*

Callanan, Mark 38
Camberwell, south London 9, 23
Cameron, David, Prime Minister
    14, 146, 147
Cameron, Gloria 46
Campbell, Alastair 122
Caribbean Commonwealth heads of
    state 171
Catford College, south London 37
Chandran Foundation 199
Chandran, Captain 148, 199
Channel 4 News 170
Chasing Status Report 176
Chelsea Football Club 35, 38, *114*,
    154, 157, 160, 161, 165, 199,
    200, 201
Childline 128
City of London 86, 90, 123, 128
Clapham Common 23, 49
Clarke, Greg 156, 157, 183, 200
Coalition Government 143, 144,
    145, 147, 184
Cohen, Barbara 125
Combat 18 107
Commission for Racial Equality
    (CRE) 45, 86, 100, *111*, 115, 144
Commonwealth Caribbean 14, 172
Commonwealth Heads of
    Government Conference 171,
    174, *175*
Community Affairs Committee,
    Lambeth Council 51, 60
Community Involvement and
    Participation Project 81
Community Involvement and
    Participation Strategy 80

Community Relations Council,
    Lambeth 44, 45, 46, 48, 51
Condon, Sir Paul 106
Confederation of Business Industry
    (CBI) 73, 110, 112
Conlon United, football team 33, 35
Conservative government 14, 117,
    184
Conservative Party 61, 76, 77, 109
Construction Industry Training
    Board (CITB) 65
Construction Services Committee 65
Cook, Tom 122
Council for Legal Education 106
Council of Jews and Christians 128
County Hall 58, 68, 69, 71, 79
Covid-19 pandemic 12, 15, 166,
    179, 183, 186
Crooks, Garth 154

Daphne (mother) 8, 19, 20, 21, 23,
    25, 26, 28, 30, *195*
Davies, David 152
Davies, Sir Howard 150
Davis, Spencer 33
Day, Michael 100, 106
Dein, David 152, 161
Dennis, George (headmaster) 26
Department of Environment 56
Desiree (sister) 19, 21
Different Realities Partnership
    133, 134
Direct Labour Organisations
    (DLOs) 95
Disability Discrimination Unit,
    Lambeth Council 81
Disability Rights Commission 144
Doris (sister) 19, 21
Douglas, Carl, friend, singer 31,
    32, 33
Downing Street 106, 122
Dulwich Hamlet Football Club 199
Dulwich, south London 9, 21, 27, 28
Dyke, Greg 156

Earl, Robbie 160
East Dulwich, south London 21
East Staffordshire REC 128
Edis, Peter 35, 36

Edwards, Martin 150
Egbert (step-father) 21
Elliott, Paul *114*, 153, 157, 160
Employment Advisory Group 128
Employment Select Committee 109
English Football League 154, 155, 180
English Heritage 128
Equality Act, 2010 145
Equality and Human Rights Commission (EHRC) 133, 144
Equality, Diversity and Inclusion Plan 183
Ethnic Minorities Committee 77
Ethnic Minorities Unit, GLC 66, 68, 69, 85
EU (European Union) Free Movement Directive 172
EU (European Union) Referendum, 2016 147
Evra, Patrice 165

Facebook 167
Fame, Georgie 33
Farage, Nigel 146
Farlow, Chris 33
Fashanu, John *114*, 154
Faulkner, Richard 114, 160
Ferdinand, Anton 165
Ferguson, Alex 160
FIFA 2018 World Cup, Russia 179
Fishwick, John 44
Flamingo Club 33
Fletcher, Neil 90
Floyd, Eddie 33
Focus Consultancy 10
Football Foundation 114, 151
Football Offences Act 154
Football Trust *114*, 151, 160
Foreign and Commonwealth Office 169, 173
Franklin, Aretha 33

Gazidis, Ivan 161
Gentleman, Amelia 170
George, Eddie 123, 128
George, John 92
Georgetown, Guyana 8, 20
German Football Association 192

Gill, David 161
Gillan, Cheryl 128
global pandemic 12, 15, 16, 177, 179, 186, 190
Greater London Authority 78
Greater London Council (GLC) 35-6, 58, 64, 66-68, 70-80, 85-6, 100, 101, 112, 118
Greaves, George 44, 46
Green Party 176
Grenfell Tower fire 174
Guthrie, General Sir Charles 123
Guyana 8, 21, 24-26, 44
Gypsy communities 75

Haque, Mr, campaigner 77
Hare, Jimmy 38
Haringey Borough Council 132
Harris, Hugh 109, 112, 131
Hastings, Michael 109
Hayes, Isaac 33
Hendrix, Jimi 32-3
Henry, Thierry 159
Her Majesty the Queen 169, 171
Hewitt, Guy 170
Heysel Stadium disaster, 1985 150
High Commissioners, Caribbean 170-173, *175*
Higher Education Funding Council 90
Hill, Ricky 154
Hollamby, Edward 38
Holman (school housemaster) 27, 28
Home Affairs Select Committee 106, 109
Home Office 48, 106, 168-177
House of Commons *121*, 174, 194, 196
House of Lords 71, 134, 171, 193, 194, *195*, 196, 199
Household Cavalry 124, 125, 126
Howard League 109
Howe, Darcus 46
Howlett, Peter 90
Hyslop, Miranda 46

Immigration Act 1971 172
Impact Statement 110
Inclusion Advisory Board 157
Indian Workers Association 109

Inner London Education Authority
    (ILEA) 85-92, 100, 112, 118
Insley, Bob 23
Instagram 167
Institute for Race Relations 148
Inter-City Inter-faith Network 128
Irish Report, University of North
    London 128
Israel, Simon 170

Jamaica 31, 46
Javid, Sajid 176, 177
Jewish Council for Racial Equality
    122
Joint Council for the Welfare of
    Immigrants (JCWI) 170
Josephine (aunt) 19, 21

Keep Britain White (KBW), graffiti 22
Keighley College 137
Khan, Omar 171
Kick It Out 114, 128, 134, 148, 153-
    166, 181, 192, 199, 200
Kinnock, Neil 94
Kirby, 'Kipper' 26
Knights, Alan 38

Labour government 14, 78, 115,
    120, 129, 143
Labour Party 53, 78, 94, 122, 132
Lambert, David 109
Lambeth Borough Council 36, 40,
    44, 51, 55, 56, 62, 79, 92, 99,
    101-5, 112, *129*
Lambeth Council Community
    Affairs Committee 51
Lambeth Law Centre 48
Lambeth Town Hall 51
Lammy, David 174, 177
Lane, David 100
Lansley, Stewart 51
Lawrence, Doreen 107, 108
Lawrence, Neville 107, 108
Lawrence, Sir Ivan 106
Lawrence, Stephen 13, 61, 107,
    108, 122, 138, 139
Laws, Courtney 46
Leadership Challenge 120, *121*, 123
League Managers' Association

(LMA) 155, 163, 180
League of Jewish Women 128
Leech, Micky 38
Leicester City Football Club 128
Let's Kick Racism Out of Football
    113, *114*, 148, 150, 160, 201
Lewisham REC 128
LGBTQ 74, 163, 183
Liberal Party 101
Littlewoods Organisation 128
Liverpool City Council 128
Liverpool Football Club 161, 165
Livingstone, Ken 66, 67, 68, 74, 78
Lloyd (work colleague) 49
Lloyd, Peter 106, 107
Local Government Management
    Diploma 37
London Against Racism, campaign
    79, *80*
London Assembly 132
London Borough of Brent 75
London Borough of Hackney 36
'London Bridge is falling down',
    nursery rhyme 8
London County Council (LCC) 35, 91
London Evening Standard 99, 105
London Fire Service 71, 72
Lucas, Caroline 176

MacIntosh, Andrew 66
Maclennan, Francis 46
Macpherson Inquiry Report 13, 14,
    61, 108, 138-145
Macpherson, Sir William 13, 122,
    143
Major, John 121
Mallen, David 90
Manchester City Football Club 150,
    199, 201
Manchester United Football Club
    35, 150, 160, 161, 165
Manchester United Foundation 182
Mandela, Nelson 128, *129*
Mandelson, Peter 122, 130
Manningham Youth Forum 128
May, Theresa, Prime Minister 14,
    168-171, 176-7
McDonnell, John 74
Melting Pot Foundation 47

Metropolitan Police (Met) 48, 106, 122-3, 128, 139, 140
Middlesex County Council 10, 34, 35, 112, 118
Millwall Football Club 23
Mings, Tyrone 167
Ministry of Defence (MoD) 125, 127
Mobile Doctors Limited 106
Money, Zoot 33
Monitoring Report, Lambeth Council 97
Morrell, Frances 88, 90
Morris, Olive 46
Morrison, Reg 65
Mortimore, Peter 88
Mullard, Professor Chris 10
Multi-Agency Forum on Racial Harassment, Wales 128

Napoli Football Club 201
Narayan, Rudy 46
National Council for Voluntary Organisations 101
National Front 68
National Health Service (NHS) 15, 45, 170, 173, 186
National Probation Service 100
Neil, Dwain 109, 125
New Cross, south London 9
New Labour 78, 122, 129, 130, 143
Newsam, Peter 86, 100
Non-discrimination Notice 124
North Dulwich station 27-8
Northern Ireland Civil Service (NICS) 136
Northern Ireland Commission for Racial Equality 116, 133
Northern Ireland Executive 135
Nunhead, south London 9, 21

O'Brien, Mike 131
Old Trafford football ground 35
Operation Swamp 50
Ottey, Tony 46
Overseas Doctors' Association 109, 128
Ozil, Mesut 191

Parliament 90, 91, 109, 134, 174, 193, 196

Parliamentary Select Committee for Culture, Media, Sport and Digital Services 157
Patel, Naina 148
Patel, Priti 177
Peckham, south London 8, 9, 21, 22, 32, 40, 68, 87
Peters, Jack 37
Peters, Terry 23, 33
Phillips, Trevor 101, *129*, 132
Pickett, Wilson 33
Pleat, David 161
Police Monitoring Committee 70
Policy and Research Institute for Ageing and Ethnicity 148
Poll Tax 93
Port of Spain, Trinidad 20
Powar, Piara 154
Powell, Enoch 45, 52, 189
Prashar, Usha 101
Premier League 152-155, 161, 164, 180, 192, 200, 201
Preset Education and Training Project 148
Pride of Britain Award 198
Prince Charles 123, 124, 128, *129*
Prince's Youth Business Trust 109, 128
Professional Footballers Association (PFA) 114, *114*, 151, 153-155, 160, 163, 200
Project Fullemploy 101
Public Sector Equality Duty 61
Purkiss, Bob 109, 125, 126, 133

Queen's Park Rangers Football Club 165

Race Disparities Audit, 2017 76
Race Equality Standard 154
Race Equality Unit, Lambeth Council 57
Race for Opportunity (RfO) 112, 128, *129*
Race Relations (Amendment) Act, 2000 61, 122, 138
Race Relations (Northern Ireland) Order 116
Race Relations Act, 1976 45, 56, 75, 110, 124, 127

Race Relations Unit, Lambeth
    Council 51-64, 67, 81
Railton Road, Brixton 51
Rashford, Marcus 167
Ray 38
Ray, Dipak 109
Red Tape Challenge 143
Redding, Otis 33
Regis, Cyril 154
Reid, Dr John 127
Respect campaign 128, 165
Rivers of Blood, speech, Enoch
    Powell 45, 52
Robertson, George 125
Robson, Sir Bobby 161
Rogers, Sheila 133
Roma communities 75
Roots of the Future 128
Royal Borough of Kensington and
    Chelsea 174
Royal Festival Hall 130
Rudd, Amber 175-177
Runnymede Trust 101, 128, 132, 171

Saatchi & Saatchi 111, *111*, 112
Sam and Dave 33
Sampson, Mark 157
Scarman, Lord 139
Scotland Yard 50
Scudamore, Richard 161, 200
Second World War 14, 19, 22, 147, *175*
Section 71, 1976 Race Relations Act 56
Select Committee on Home Affairs
    106, 109
Selhurst Park 160
Senior Civil Service (SCS) 135-6
Sentamu, Dr John 122
Shepherd's Bush, west London 75
Shergold, Vernon 40
Shipley College 137
Show Racism the Red Card 159, 163
Shreeves, Peter 161
Sid (work colleague) 48-50
Silverstone, Daniel 58, 64
Simister, Clive 31
Singh, Gurbux 132
Singh, Raminder 106
Singh, Satbir 170
Smith, John 34

Snapchat 167
Soho, London 32-3
Solicitors Regulatory Authority
    (SRA) 141-2
South Bank Centre 130
South London Press 96
Southgate, Gareth 180
Special Patrol Group (SPG) 50
Spencer, Linbert 101
Spud 38
SS Italia, cargo and passenger
    liner 20
St James's Palace 124
St Kitts and Nevis High
    Commission 173, *175*
St Saviours, local parish church 23, 30
Stamford Bridge 199
Stein brothers, professional
    footballers 154
Stephen Lawrence Inquiry Report
    13, 61, 122, 138-9
Sterling, Raheem 167, 199, 201
Stevens, Sir John 139, 140
Stewart, Rod 33
Stone, Dr Richard 122
Straw, Jack 108, 115, 122, 129, 139
Stubbs, William 87, 90
Suarez, Luis 161, 165
Sure-Start 144, 184
Swaffield, Sir James 86

Taylor, Gordon *114*, 151, 160
Taylor, Graham 161
Terry, John 165
Thakker, Jay 46
Thamesmead 77
Thatcher, Margaret 52, 83, 189
The Bag O'Nails, London 32-3
The Guardian 130, 170
Thea, Dan 62, 64
Thorpe, Jeremy 101
Tottenham, north London 14
Traveller communities 75
Treasury 102, 177, 179
Treisman, David 156
Trooping the Colour 125
Trotter, John 37, 103
TUC (Trades Union Congress) 110,
    112

Turner, Alan 37
Twitter 167
Two Nations concert, Albert Hall 128

UEFA 150
UKIP 146
UNICEF 183
United States (USA) 15, 21, 33, 71,
    146

Vieira, Patrick 159

Wandsworth Council 61
Watkins, Alan 23, 33
Webb, Rene 46, 47
Weekly Journal 101
Weleminsky, Judy 46
Wells, Mary 64
Welsh Language Board 128
Wenger, Arsene 161
West Indies Test cricket team 25
West London Synagogue 109
West Yorkshire Police 137
West, Chris 38, 103
Westway Traveller site, west
    London 75
Whaley, Steve 96
White City, west London 75
William Penn Secondary School,
    Dulwich 21, 23, 27, 38
Wiltshire, Bernard 88
Wimbledon Football Club *114*, 160
Windrush Generation 44, 47, 173-
    177
Windrush scandal 14, *175*
Windsor Fellowship 128
Women's Unit, Lambeth Council 81
Wonder, Stevie 79, *80*
Wong, Ansel 46
Woody 38

'Yes Minister', 1980s TV political
    sitcom 16
Yorkshire Forward 137
Youth Chamber for Sport 128
YouTube 167